The

Three Charters

of the

Virginia Company of London

With Seven Related Documents; 1606-1621

Samuel M. Bemiss

CLEARFIELD

Originally published
1957

Reprinted for
Clearfield Company by
Genealogical Publishing Co.
Baltimore, Maryland
1993, 2007

ISBN-13: 978-0-8063-5088-2
ISBN-10: 0-8063-5088-1

Made in the United States of America

Jamestown 350th Anniversary Historical Booklet
Number 4

CONTENTS

INTRODUCTION

Historians may trace in the Royal charters issued to the Virginia Company of London a course of empire; a Company organized for profit by the ablest businessmen of their time—merchants, manufacturers, statesmen, and artists who bound themselves together in a joint stock enterprise. The historian may also find in the three charters here published a pattern for a parliamentary system and its development into the American form of government. He might even perceive the inception of a new society.

The origin of the joint stock company was probably primitive. Its later genesis may readily be seen in the medieval guild. It became an English institution in its application by Sir Walter Raleigh to his magnificent adventures in both honest trade and romantic piracy.

The Company provided an agency for assembling adventure capital and supplying able management to enterprises of great moment. It offered an invitation to the industrious to participate in the growing wealth and expanding power of the great English middle class. It supplied an opportunity to small investors and it limited their liability. It was an adaptation by practical people to practical problems.

Subscribers, or shareholders, met in their quarterly courts to discuss the business of the Company and participate in its management. These courts were the counterpart of our present day corporate stockholders' meetings and were characterized by the same sort of discussions. King James could protest vehemently against the "democratical principles of the Company." He could see in their charters the final death warrant of feudalism. He could execute Raleigh "chiefly for giving satisfaction to the King of Spain." He could revoke the charters in 1624, but he could not stop the rising tide of representative institutions nor darken the great vision of the liberal Elizabethans. A new day had dawned.

The General Assembly which met at Jamestown in 1619 was the natural child of the Company. Some of the planters along the James River were shareholders in the Company. They had a voice in its management. In the management of the civil affairs of the Colony it was, therefore, logical that the plantations should elect their representatives to the local governing body, It was thus that the first freely elected parliament of a self-governing people in the Western World came into existence. Its principles were based on those of the corporation chartered and organized for profit by businessmen.

The three charters here published, changed successively to meet changing conditions, were the rules and the by-laws for the commercial, economic, and political development of a homogeneous, industrious English society in a land of opportunity. The principal authors and executors of the charters, Sir Thomas Smith and Sir Edwin and George Sandys, were businessmen. They were practical men. They found a practical way to assemble capital and ability, and coordinate them in constructive enterprise.

A hundred years before the great Virginia adventure, Luther, Erasmus, and Columbus rang down the curtain on the weary and confined drama of the Middle Ages. Expanding horizons challenged man's vision and intellect. Great courage made Englishmen adventurers in all things.

The charters here presented are among the world's great documents. The first which was drawn while Sir Edward Coke was Lord Chief Justice is replete with certain traditional and feudal principles, reverence for the English common law and the supreme authority of the King and his agents. The second, principally the work of the liberal Sir Edwin Sandys with the approving participation of Sir Francis Bacon, great exponent of natural law, marks a transition from government by arbitrary royal authority to the concept that government rests on the consent of the governed and on the fundamental right of man to enjoy the fruits of his labor. Students may read in this charter the first principles of the American Constitution. The third charter is an attempt to refine principles enunciated in the second in the light of experience. In addition to its political significance, the second charter proved a tremendous stimulus to the Virginia enterprise.

Gondomar, the Spanish Ambassador, wrote to his King that "fourteen Counts and Barons have given 40,000 ducats, the merchants give much more and there is no poor little man or woman who is not willing to subscribe something." The landed aristocracy, gentry, merchants, and yeomen had joined in a company which they directed to provide capital and ability for a great enterprise.

The text of the three charters of the Virginia Company is taken from a contemporary copy recently discovered among the Chancery Rolls of the Public Record Office in London—contemporary enrollments "representing the official text of the charters kept in official custody," according to the Deputy Keeper, Mr. D. L. Evans. A photostatic copy of this manuscript is in possession of the Virginia State Library. Each charter was transcribed in England by Doctor Nellie J. M. Kerling for the editor's use.

Heretofore scholars have had access to the charters only through the text in William Stith's *The History of the First Discovery and Settlement of Virginia* (Williamsburg, Printed by William Parks, 1747), in sources based upon this, or in Alexander Brown's *The Genesis of the United States* (Boston, 1890).

No original of any of the charters is known to exist, although other copies of varying degrees of completeness have been located in England and on the continent. One copy, made with the authority of the Governor, Council, and House of Burgesses of the Colony, was used as evidence to support a petition against Lord Culpeper's land grants. This is included in the Henry Coventry papers in the library of the Marquess of Bath at Longleat, Wiltshire, England (Vol. LXXVI, *Papers relating to Virginia, Barbados, and other Colonies, 1606-1675*). These documents have been microfilmed by the American Council of Learned Societies, "British Manuscripts Project." Many of them will soon be published by the Virginia Historical Society under the editorship of Dr. W. E. Washburn.

Another copy of the charters is in the Public Record Office, "Entry books of letters, commissions, instructions, charters, warrants, patents, grants, etc." (formerly "Record book No. LXXIX"), an abstract of which appears in the *Calendar of State Papers, Colonial Series,* Vol. I. Microfilm copies of this text are in the Library of Congress and the Virginia State Library. Other copies have recently been discovered in France and Spain by Dr. George Reese who has been employed by the Virginia 350th Anniversary Celebration Corporation to search foreign libraries for documentary material pertinent to the study of 17th century Virginia. Ultimately, microfilm copies of these records will be made available to research libraries in the United States.

The seven accompanying documents, included to illustrate the practical rather than theoretical basis of the administration of the Colony, have been taken from the best available manuscript or printed source. These official papers, together with the three charters of the Virginia Company, may be termed the constitutions and are the basic sources for the study of the Colony during the first fifteen years of its existence.

A few necessary liberties have been taken in transcribing these documents: abbreviations and contractions have been spelled out, capitalization and punctuation have been adjusted according to modern usage and, to prevent possible confusion, certain letters used interchangeably (such as "i" and "j", "v" and "u") are employed according to twentieth century practice. In the text of the three charters, omitted words or phrases have been supplied in brackets from the text in Stith. Brackets are also employed to supply the name of an adventurer if there is any deviation in spelling between Stith and the manuscript version: *e.g.*, "Sir Charles Willmott, Knight [Wilmot]."

This publication owes its issuance to the inspiration and leadership furnished by Dr. Earl G. Swem, Librarian Emeritus of the College of William and Mary. I should like also to acknowledge the faithful transcription of the text by Dr. Nellie J. N. Kerling, and the deep interest and active support of Dr. Gertrude R. B. Richards, who most patiently assisted in the transcription; also to Mr. Francis L. Berkeley, Jr., Archivist of the Alderman Library, University of Virginia and to Mr. John M. Jennings, Director of the Virginia Historical Society. To Mr. James A. Servies, Reference Librarian of the Library of William and Mary College, has fallen the arduous and difficult task of a comparative, detailed study of all the texts in the different versions. The printed text in these pages is from a typed copy by Mr. Servies, prepared with the most painstaking application, as the result of the comparison of copies transcribed by Dr. Kerling and Dr. Richards, and of the printed pages in Stith. The merit of an accurate and readable text must be ascribed to the industry and scholarly perception of Mr. Servies.

SAMUEL M. BEMISS

THE THREE CHARTERS OF THE VIRGINIA COMPANY OF LONDON

THE FIRST CHARTER

April 10, 1606

James, by the grace of God [King of England, Scotland, France, and Ireland, Defender of the Faith], etc. Whereas our loving and weldisposed subjects, Sir Thomas Gates and Sir George Somers, Knightes; Richarde Hackluit, Clarke, Prebendarie of Westminster; and Edwarde Maria Winghfeilde,[1] Thomas Hannam and Raleighe Gilberde, Esquiers; William Parker and George Popham, Gentlemen; and divers others of our loving subjects, have been humble sutors unto us that wee woulde vouchsafe unto them our licence to make habitacion, plantacion and to deduce a colonie of sondrie of our people into that parte of America commonly called Virginia, and other parts and territories in America either appartaining unto us or which are not nowe actuallie possessed by anie Christian prince or people, scituate, lying and being all along the sea coastes between fower and thirtie degrees of northerly latitude from the equinoctiall line and five and fortie degrees of the same latitude and in the maine lande betweene the same fower and thirtie and five and fourtie degrees, and the ilandes thereunto adjacente or within one hundred miles of the coaste thereof;

And to that ende, and for the more speedy accomplishemente of theire saide intended plantacion and habitacion there, are desirous to devide themselves into two severall colonies and companies, the one consisting of certaine Knightes, gentlemen, marchanntes and other adventurers of our cittie of London, and elsewhere, which are and from time to time shalbe joined unto them which doe desire to begin theire plantacions and habitacions in some fitt and conveniente place between fower and thirtie and

[1]Throughout, this and the following two names are spelled as "Wingfield," "Hanham," and "Gilbert" in Stith.

one and fortie degrees of the said latitude all alongest the coaste of Virginia and coastes of America aforesaide; and the other consisting of sondrie Knightes, gentlemen, merchanntes, and other adventurers of our citties of Bristoll and Exeter, and of our towne of Plymouthe, and of other places which doe joine themselves unto that colonie which doe desire to beginn theire plantacions and habitacions in some fitt and convenient place betweene eighte and thirtie degrees and five and fortie degrees of the saide latitude all alongst the saide coaste of Virginia and America as that coaste lieth;

Wee, greately commending and graciously accepting of theire desires to the furtherance of soe noble a worke which may, by the providence of Almightie God, hereafter tende to the glorie of His Divine Majestie in propagating of Christian religion to suche people as yet live in darkenesse and miserable ignorance of the true knoweledge and worshippe of God and may in tyme bring the infidels and salvages living in those parts to humane civilitie and to a setled and quiet govermente, doe by theise our lettres patents graciously accepte of and agree to theire humble and well intended desires;

And doe, therefore, for us, our heires and successors, grannte and agree that the saide Sir Thomas Gates, Sir George Sumers, Richarde Hackluit and Edwarde Maria Winghfeilde, adventurers of and for our cittie of London, and all suche others as are or shalbe joined unto them of that Colonie, shalbe called the Firste Colonie, and they shall and may beginne theire saide firste plantacion and seate of theire firste aboade and habitacion at anie place upon the saide coaste of Virginia or America where they shall thincke fitt and conveniente betweene the saide fower and thirtie and one and fortie degrees of the saide latitude; and that they shall have all the landes, woods, soile, groundes, havens, ports, rivers, mines, mineralls, marshes, waters, fishinges, commodities and hereditamentes whatsoever, from the said first seate of theire plantacion and habitacion by the space of fiftie miles of Englishe statute measure all alongest the saide coaste of Virginia and America towardes the weste and southe weste as the coaste lieth, with all the islandes within one hundred miles directlie over againste the same sea coaste; and alsoe all the landes, soile, groundes, havens, ports, rivers, mines, mineralls, woods, marrishes [marshes], waters, fishinges, commodities and hereditamentes whatsoever, from the saide place of theire firste plantacion and habitacion for the space of fiftie like Englishe miles, all alongest the saide coaste of Virginia and America towardes the easte and northeaste [or toward the north] as the coaste lieth, together with all the islandes within one hundred miles directlie over againste the same sea coaste; and alsoe all the landes, woodes, soile, groundes, havens, portes, rivers, mines, mineralls, marrishes, waters, fishinges, commodities and hereditamentes whatsoever, from the same fiftie miles everie waie on the sea coaste directly into the maine lande by the space of one hundred like Englishe miles; and shall and may inhabit and remaine there; and shall and may alsoe builde and fortifie within anie the same for theire better safegarde and defence, according to theire best discrecions and the direction of the Counsell of that Colonie; and that noe other of our subjectes shalbe permitted or suffered to plante or inhabit behinde or on the backside of them towardes the maine lande, without the expresse licence or consente of the Counsell of that Colonie thereunto in writing firste had or obtained.

And wee doe likewise for us, our heires and successors, by theise presentes grannte and agree that the saide Thomas Hannam and Raleighe Gilberde, William Parker and George Popham, and all others of the towne of Plymouthe in the countie of Devon, or elsewhere, which are or shalbe joined unto them of that Colonie, shalbe called the Seconde Colonie; and that they shall and may beginne theire saide firste plantacion and seate of theire first aboade and habitacion at anie place upon the saide coaste of Virginia and America, where they shall thincke fitt and conveniente, betweene eighte and thirtie degrees of the saide latitude and five and fortie degrees of the same latitude; and that they shall have all the landes, soile, groundes, havens, ports, rivers, mines, mineralls, woods, marishes, waters, fishinges, commodities and hereditaments whatsoever, from the firste seate of theire plantacion and habitacion by the space of fiftie like Englishe miles, as is aforesaide, all alongeste the saide coaste of Virginia and America towardes the weste and southwest, or towardes the southe, as the coaste lieth, and all the islandes within one hundred miles directlie over againste the saide sea coaste; and alsoe all the landes, soile, groundes, havens, portes, rivers, mines, mineralls, woods, marishes, waters, fishinges, commodities and hereditamentes whatsoever, from the saide place of theire firste plantacion and habitacion for the space of fiftie like miles all alongest the saide coaste of Virginia and America towardes the easte and northeaste or towardes the northe, as the coaste liethe, and all the islandes alsoe within one hundred miles directly over againste the same sea coaste; and alsoe all the landes, soile, groundes, havens, ports, rivers, woodes, mines, mineralls, marishes, waters, fishings, commodities and hereditaments whatsoever, from the same fiftie miles everie waie on the sea coaste, directlie into the maine lande by the space of one hundred like Englishe miles; and shall and may inhabit and remaine there; and shall and may alsoe builde and fortifie within anie the same for theire better saufegarde according to theire beste discrecions and the direction of the Counsell of that Colonie; and that none of our subjectes shalbe permitted or suffered to plante or inhabit behinde or on the backe of them towardes the maine lande without the expresse licence or consente of the Counsell of that Colonie, in writing thereunto, firste had and obtained.

Provided alwaies, and our will and pleasure herein is, that the plantacion and habitacion of suche of the saide Colonies as shall laste plante themselves, as aforesaid, shall not be made

Photo by T. L. Williams

King James I
from the painting by Paul Van Somer

within one hundred like Englishe miles of the other of them that firste beganne to make theire plantacion, as aforesaide.

And wee doe alsoe ordaine, establishe and agree for [us], our heires and successors, that eache of the saide Colonies shall have a Counsell which shall governe and order all matters and causes which shall arise, growe, or happen to or within the same severall Colonies, according to such lawes, ordinannces and instructions as shalbe in that behalfe, given and signed with our hande or signe manuell and passe under the Privie Seale of our realme of Englande; eache of which Counsells shall consist of thirteene parsons[2] and to be ordained, made and removed from time to time according as shalbe directed and comprised in the same instructions; and shall have a severall seale for all matters that shall passe or concerne the same severall Counsells, eache of which seales shall have the Kinges armes engraven on the one side there of and his pourtraiture on the other; and that the seale for the Counsell of the saide Firste Colonie shall have engraven rounde about on the one side theise wordes: Sigillum Regis Magne Britanie, Francie [et] Hibernie; on the other side this inscripture rounde about: Pro Consillio Prime Colonie Virginie. And the seale for the Counsell of the saide Seconde Colonie shall alsoe have engraven rounde about the one side thereof the foresaide wordes: Sigillum Regis Magne Britanie, Francie [et] Hibernie; and on the other side: Pro Consilio Secunde Colonie Virginie.

And that alsoe ther shalbe a Counsell established here in Englande which shall in like manner consist of thirteen parsons to be, for that purpose, appointed by us, our heires and successors, which shalbe called our Counsell of Virginia; and shall from time to time have the superior managing and direction onelie of and for all matters that shall or may concerne the govermente, as well of the said severall Colonies as of and for anie other parte

[2] *i.e.*, "persons"

or place within the aforesaide precinctes of fower and thirtie and five and fortie degrees abovementioned; which Counsell shal in like manner have a seale for matters concerning the Counsell [or Colonies] with the like armes and purtraiture as aforesaide, with this inscription engraven rounde about the one side: Sigillum Regis Magne Britanie, Francie [et] Hibernie; and rounde about the other side: Pro Consilio Suo Virginie.

And more over wee doe grannte and agree for us, our heires and successors, that the saide severall Counsells of and for the saide severall Colonies shall and lawfully may by vertue hereof, from time to time, without interuption of us, our heires or successors, give and take order to digg, mine and searche for all manner of mines of goulde, silver and copper, as well within anie parte of theire saide severall Colonies as of the saide maine landes on the backside of the same Colonies; and to have and enjoy the goulde, silver and copper to be gotten there of to the use and behoofe of the same Colonies and the plantacions thereof; yeilding therefore yerelie to us, our heires and successors, the fifte parte onelie of all the same goulde and silver and the fifteenth parte of all the same copper soe to be gotten or had, as is aforesaid, and without anie other manner of profitt or accompte to be given or yeilded to us, our heires or successors, for or in respecte of the same.

And that they shall or lawfullie may establishe and cawse to be made a coine, to passe currant there betwene the people of those severall Colonies for the more ease of traffique and bargaining betweene and amongest them and the natives there, of such mettall and in such manner and forme as the same severall Counsells there shall limitt and appointe. And wee doe likewise for us, our heires and successors, by theise presents give full power and auctoritie to the said Sir Thomas Gates, Sir George Sumers, Richarde Hackluit, Edwarde Maria Winghfeilde, Thomas Hannam, Raleighe Gilberde, William Parker and George Popham, and to everie of them, and to the saide severall Companies, plantacions and Colonies, that they and everie of them shall and may at all and everie time and times hereafter have, take and leade in the saide voyage, and for and towardes the saide severall plantacions and Colonies, and to travell thitherwarde and to abide and inhabit there in everie of the saide Colonies and plantacions, such and somanie of our subjectes as shall willinglie accompanie them, or anie of them, in the saide voyages and plantacions, with sufficiente shipping and furniture of armour, weapon, ordonnance, powder, victall, and all other thinges necessarie for the saide plantacions and for theire use and defence there: provided alwaies that none of the said parsons be such as hereafter shalbe speciallie restrained by us, our heires or successors.

Moreover, wee doe by theise presents, for us, our heires and successors, give and grannte licence unto the said Sir Thomas Gates, Sir George Sumers, Richarde Hackluite, Edwarde Maria Winghfeilde, Thomas Hannam, Raleighe Gilberde, William Parker and George Popham, and to everie of the said Colinies, that they and everie of them shall and may, from time to time and at all times for ever hereafter, for theire severall defences, incounter or expulse, repell and resist, aswell by sea as by lande, by all waies and meanes whatsoever, all and everie suche parson and parsons as without espiciall licence of the said severall Colonies and plantacions shall attempte to inhabit within the saide severall precincts and limitts of the saide severall Colonies and plantacions, or anie of them, or that shall enterprise or attempt at anie time hereafter the hurte, detrimente or annoyance of the saide severall Colonies or plantacions.

Giving and grannting by theise presents unto the saide Sir Thomas Gates, Sir George Somers, Richarde Hackluite, and Edwarde Maria Winghfeilde, and theire associates of the said Firste Colonie, and unto the said Thomas Hannam, Raleighe Gilberde, William Parker and George Popham, and theire associates of the saide Second Colonie, and to everie of them from time to time and at all times for ever hereafter, power and auctoritie to take and surprize by all waies and meanes whatsoever all and everie parson and parsons with theire shipps, vessels, goods and other furniture, which shalbe founde traffiqueing into anie harbor or harbors, creeke, creekes or place within the limitts or precincts of the saide severall Colonies and plantacions, not being of the same Colonie, untill such time as they, being of anie realmes or dominions under our obedience, shall paie or agree to paie to the handes of the Tresorer of the Colonie, within whose limitts and precincts theie shall soe traffique, twoe and a halfe upon anie hundred of anie thing soe by them traffiqued, boughte or soulde; and being stranngers and not subjects under our obeysannce, untill they shall paie five upon everie hundred of suche wares and commoditie as theie shall traffique, buy or sell within the precincts of the saide severall Colonies wherein theie shall soe traffique, buy or sell, as aforesaide; which sommes of money or benefitt, as aforesaide, for and during the space of one and twentie yeres nexte ensuing the date hereof shalbe whollie imploied to the use, benefitt and behoofe of the saide severall plantacions where such trafficque shalbe made; and after the saide one and twentie yeres ended the same shalbe taken to the use of us, our heires and successors by such officer and minister as by us, our heires and successors shalbe thereunto assigned or appointed.

And wee doe further, by theise presentes, for us, our heires and successors, give and grannte unto the saide Sir Thomas Gates, Sir George Sumers, Richarde Hachluit, and Edwarde Maria Winghfeilde, and to theire associates of the saide Firste Colonie and plantacion, and to the saide Thomas Hannam, Raleighe Gilberde, William Parker and George Popham, and theire associates of the saide Seconde Colonie and plantacion, that theie and everie of them by theire deputies, ministers and factors may transport the goods, chattells, armor, munition and furniture, needfull to be used by them for theire saide apparrell, defence or otherwise in respecte of the saide plantacions, out of our realmes of Englande and Irelande and all other our dominions from time to time, for and during the time of seaven yeres nexte ensuing the date hereof for the better releife of the said severall Colonies and plantacions, without anie custome, subsidie or other dutie unto us, our heires or successors to be yeilded or paide for the same.

Alsoe wee doe, for us, our heires and successors, declare by theise presentes that all and everie the parsons being our subjects which shall dwell and inhabit within everie or anie of the saide severall Colonies and plantacions and everie of theire children which shall happen to be borne within the limitts and precincts of the said severall Colonies and plantacions shall have and enjoy all liberties, franchises and immunites within anie of our other dominions to all intents and purposes as if they had been abiding and borne within this our realme of Englande or anie other of our saide dominions.

Moreover our gracious will and pleasure is, and wee doe by theise presents, for us, our heires and successors, declare and sett forthe, that if anie parson or parsons which shalbe of anie of the said Colonies and plantacions or anie other, which shall trafficque to the saide Colonies and plantacions or anie of them, shall at anie time or times hereafter transporte anie wares, marchandize or commodities out of [any] our dominions with a pretence and purpose to lande, sell or otherwise dispose the same within anie the limitts and precincts of anie of the saide Colonies and plantacions, and yet nevertheles being at the sea or after he hath landed the same within anie of the said Colonies and plantacions, shall carrie the same into any other forraine countrie with a purpose there to sell or dispose of the same without the licence of us, our heires or successors in that behalfe first had or obtained, that then all the goods and chattels of the saide parson or parsons soe offending and transporting, together with the said shippe or vessell wherein suche transportacion was made, shall be forfeited to us, our heires and successors.

Provided alwaies, and our will and pleasure is and wee doe hereby declare to all Christian kinges, princes and estates, that if anie parson or parsons which shall hereafter be of anie of the said severall Colonies and plantacions, or anie other, by his, theire, or anie of theire licence or appointment, shall at anie time or times hereafter robb or spoile by sea or by lande or doe anie acte of unjust and unlawfull hostilitie to anie the subjects of us, our heires or successors, or anie of the subjects of anie king, prince, ruler, governor or state being then in league or amitie with us, our heires or successors, and that upon suche injurie or upon juste complainte of such prince, ruler, governor or state or their subjects, wee, our heires or successors, shall make open proclamation within anie the ports of our realme of Englande, commodious for that purpose, that the saide parson or parsons having committed anie such robberie or spoile shall, within the terme to be limitted by suche proclamations, make full restitucion or satisfaction of all suche injuries done, soe as the saide princes or others soe complained may houlde themselves fully satisfied and contented; and that if the saide parson or parsons having committed such robberie or spoile shall not make or cause to be made satisfaction accordingly with[in] such time soe to be limitted, that then it shalbe lawfull to us, our heires and successors to put the saide parson or parsons having committed such robberie or spoile and theire procurers, abbettors or comfortors out of our allegeannce and protection; and that it shalbe lawefull and free for all princes and others to pursue with hostilitie the saide offenders and everie of them and theire and everie of theire procurors, aiders, abbettors and comforters in that behalfe.

And finallie wee doe, for us, our heires and successors, grannte and agree, to and with the saide Sir Thomas Gates, Sir George Sumers, Richarde Hackluit and Edwarde Maria Winghfeilde, and all other of the saide Firste Colonie, that wee, our heires or successors, upon peticion in that behalfe to be made, shall, by lettres patents under the Greate [Seale] of Englande, give and grannte unto such parsons, theire heires and assignees, as the Counsell of that Colonie or the most part of them shall for that purpose nomminate and assigne, all the landes, tenements and hereditaments which shalbe within the precincts limitted for that Colonie, as is aforesaid, to be houlden of us, our heires and successors as of our mannor of Eastgreenwiche in the countie of Kente, in free and common soccage onelie and not in capite.

And doe, in like manner, grannte and agree, for us, our heires and successors, to and with the saide Thomas Hannam, Raleighe Gilberd, William Parker and George Popham, and all others of the saide Seconde Colonie, that wee, our heires [and] successors, upon petition in that behalfe to be made, shall, by lettres patentes under the Great Seale of Englande, give and grannte unto such parsons, theire heires and assignees, as the Counsell of that Colonie or the most parte of them shall for that purpose nomminate and assigne, all the landes, tenementes and hereditaments which shalbe within the precinctes limitted for that Colonie as is afore said, to be houlden of us, our heires and successors as of our mannor of Eastgreenwich in the countie of Kente, in free and common soccage onelie and not in capite.

All which landes, tenements and hereditaments soe to be passed by the saide severall lettres patents, shalbe, by sufficient assurances from the same patentees, soe distributed and devided amongest the undertakers for the plantacion of the said severall Colonies, and such as shall make theire plantacion in either of the said severall Colonies, in such manner and forme and for such estates as shall [be] ordered and sett [downe] by the Counsell of the same Colonie, or the most part of them, respectively, within which the same lands, tenements and hereditaments shall ly or be. Althoughe expresse mencion [of the true yearly value or certainty of the premises, or any of them, or of any other gifts or grants, by us or any our progenitors or predecessors, to the aforesaid Sir Thomas Gates, Knt. Sir George Somers, Knt. Richard Hackluit, Edward-Maria Wingfield, Thomas Hanham,

Ralegh Gilbert, William Parker, and George Popham, or any of them, heretofore made, in these presents, is not made; or any statute, act, ordnance, or provision, proclamation, or restraint, to the contrary hereof had, made, ordained, or any other thing, cause, or matter whatsoever, in any wise notwithstanding.] In witnesse whcrof [we have caused these our letters to be made patents;] witnesse our selfe at Westminister the xth day of Aprill [1606, in the fourth year of our reign of England, France, and Ireland, and of Scotland the nine and thirtieth.]

[Lukin]

Exactum per breve de private sigillo [etc.]

P. R. O. Chancery Patent Rolls (c. 66), 1709; Stith, Appendix, pp. 1-8; Hening's *Statutes*, Vol. I, pp. 57-66.

ARTICLES, INSTRUCTIONS AND ORDERS

November 20, 1606

Articles, instructions and orders made, sett down and established by us the twentieth day of November, in the year of our raigne of England, France and Ireland the fourth and of Scotland the fortieth, for the good order and government of the two several Colonies and plantations to be made by our loving subjects in the country commonly called Virginia and America, between 34 and 45 degrees from the aequinoctial line.

Wheras wee, by our letters pattents under our Great Seale of England bearing date att Westminster the tenth day of Aprill in the year of our raigne of England, France and Ireland the fourth and of Scotland the 39th, have given lycence to sundry our loving subjects named in the said letters pattents, and to their associates, to deduce and conduct two several Collonies or plantations of sundry our loving people willing to abide and inhabit in certaine parts of Virginia and America, with divers prehemminences, priviledges, authorities and other things, as in and by the same letters pattents more particularly it appeareth; wee, according to the effect and true meaning of the same letters pattents, doe by these presents, signed with our hand, signe manuel and sealed with our Privy Seale of our realme of England, establish and ordaine that our trusty and welbeloved Sir William Wade, Knight, our Lieutanant of our Tower of London; Sir Thomas Smith, Knight; Sir Walter Cope, Knight; Sir George Moor, Knight; Sir Francis Popeham, Knight; Sir Ferdinando Gorges, Knight; Sir John Trevor, Knight; Sir Henry Montague, Knight, Recorder of the city of London; Sir William Rumney, Knight; John Dodderidge, Esq., Sollicitor General; Thomas la Warr, Esq.; John Eldred, of the citty of London, merchant; Thomas James, of the citty of Bristol, merchant; and James Bagge, of Plymouth, in the county of Devonshire, merchant;

shall be our Councel for all matters which shall happen in Virginia or any the territories of America between 34 and 45 degrees from the aequinoctial line northward and the islands to the several Collonies limitted and assigned; and that they shal be called the King's Councel of Virginia, which Councel or the most part of them shal have full power and authority att our pleasure, in our name and under us, our heires and successors, to give directions to the Councels of the several Colonies which shal be within any part of the said country of Virginia and America within the degrees first above mentioned, with the islands aforesaid, for the good government of the people to be planted in those parts and for the good ordering and disposing of all causes happening within the same (and the same to be done for the substance thereof as neer to the common lawes of England and the equity thereof as may be) and to passe under our seale app[ointed][8] for that Councel, which Councel and every or any of them shall from time to [time] be increased, altered or changed and others put in their places att the [nomi]nation of us, our heires and successors and att our and their will and plea[sure]; and the same Councel of Virginia or the more part of them, for the time bei[ng], shall nominate and appoint the first several Councellours of those several Councells which are to be appointed for those two several Colonies whi[ch are] to be made plantations in Virginia and America between the degrees [before] mentioned, according to our said letters pattents in that behalfe made; and that each of the same Councels of the same several Colonies shal, by the major part of them, choose one of the same Councel, not being the minister of God's word, to be President of the same Councel and to continue in that office by the space of one whole year, unlesse he shall in the mean time dye or be removed from that office; and wee doe further hereby establish & ordaine that it shal be lawful for the

[8]The following words or letters missing from the manuscript have been supplied from the text in Hening.

major part of either of the said Councells, upon any just cause, either absence or otherwise, to remove the President or any other of that Councel from being either President or any of that Councel, and upon the deathes or removal of any of the Presidents or Councel it shal be lawfull for the major part of that Councel to elect another in the place of the party soe dying or removed, soo alwaies as they shal not be above thirteen of either of the said Councellours; and wee doe establish & ordaine that the President shal not continue in his office of Presidentship above the space of one year; and wee doe especially ordaine, charge and require the said Presidents and Councells and the ministers of the said several Colonies respectively, within their several limits and precincts, that they with all diligence, care and respect doe provide that the true word and service of God and Christian faith be preached, planted and used, not only within every of the said several Colonies and plantations but alsoe as much as they may amongst the salvage people which doe or shall adjoine unto them or border upon them, according to the doctrine, rights and religion now professed and established within our realme of England; and that they shall not suffer any person or persons to withdrawe any of the subjects or people inhabiting or which shall inhabit within any of the said several Colonies and plantations from the same or from their due allegiance unto us, our heires and successors, as their immediate soveraigne under God; and if they shall find within any of the said Colonies and plantations any person or persons soe seeking to withdrawe any of the subjects of us, our heires or successors, or any of the people of those lands or territories within the precincts aforesaid, they shall with all diligence him or them soe offending cause to be apprehended, arrested and imprisoned until he shall fully and throughly reforme himselfe, or otherwise, when the cause soe requireth, that he shall withall convenient speed be sent into our realme of England, here to receive condigne punishment for his or their said offence or offences; and moreover wee doe hereby ordaine and establish for us, our heires and successors that all the lands, tenements and hereditaments to be had and enjoyed by any of our subjects with the precincts aforesaid shal be had and inherited and injoyed according as in the like estates they be had & enjoyed by the lawes within this realme of England; and that the offences of tumults, rebellion, conspiracies, mutiny and seditions in those parts which maybe dangerous to the estates there, together with murther, manslaughter, incest, rapes and adulteries committed in those parts within the precincts of any the degrees above mentioned (and noe other offences) shal be punished by death, and that without the benefit of the clergy except in case of manslaughter, in which clergie is to be allowed; and that the said several Presidents and Councells and the greater number of them within every of the several limits and precincts shall have full power and authority to hear and determine all and every the offences aforesaid within the precinct of their several Colonies, in manner and forme following, that is to say, by twelve honest and indifferent persons sworne upon the Evangelists, to be returned by such ministers and officers, as every of the said Presidents and Councells, or the most part of them respectively, shall assigne; and the twelve persons soe returned and sworne shall, according to their evidence to be given unto them upon oath and according to the truth in their consciences, either convict or acquit every of the said persons soe to be accused & tried by them; and that all and every person or persons which shall voluntarily confesse any of the said offences to be committed by him shall, upon such his confession thereof, be convicted of the same as if he had been found guilty of the same by the verdict of any such twelve jurors, as is aforesaid; and that every person and persons which shall be accused of any of the said offences and which shall stand mute or refusing to make direct answer thereunto, shall be and be held convicted of the said offence as if he had been found guilty by the verdict of such twelve jurors, as aforesaid; and that every person and persons soe convicted

Great Seal of James I.

(A.D. 1603–1625.)

Photo by T. L. Williams

either by verdict, his own confession or by standing mute or by refusing directly to answer as aforesaid of any of the offences before mentioned, the said Presidents or Councells, or the greatest number of them within their several precincts and limitts where such conviction shall be had and made, as aforesaid, shall have full power and authority by these presents to give judgment of death upon every such offended [offender] without the benefit of the clergy, except only in cause of manslaughter, and noe person soe adjudged, attainted or condemned shall be reprived from the execution of the said judgment without the consent of the said President and Councel, or the most part of them by whom such judgment shall be given; and that noe person shal receive any pardon or be absolutely discharged of any the said offences for which he shall be condemned to death, as aforesaid, but by pardon of us, our heires and successors, under the Great Seale of England; and wee doe in like manner establish and ordaine if any either of the said Collonies shall offend in any of the offences before mentioned, within any part between the degrees aforesaid, out of the precincts of his or their Collony, that then every such offender or offenders shall be tried and punished as aforesaid within his or their proper Colony; and that every the said Presidents and Councells, within their several limits and precincts and the more part of them, shall have power and authority by these presents to hear and determine all and every other wrongs, trespasses, offences and misdemeanors whatsoever, other than those before mentioned, upon accusation of any person and proofe thereof made by sufficient witnesse upon oath; and that in all those cases the said President and Councel, and the greater number of them, shall have power and authority by these presents respectively, as is aforesaid, to punish the offender or offenders, either by reasonable corporal punishment and imprisonment or else by a convenient fine, awarding damages, or other satisfaction to the party grieved, as to the said President & Councel or to the more part of them shall be thought fitt and convenient, having regard to the quality of the offence or state of the cause; and that alsoe the said President & Councel shall have power and authority by virtue of these presents to punish all manner of excesse, through drunkennesse or otherwaies, and all idle, loytering and vagrant persons which shall be found within their several limits and precincts, according to their best discretions and with such convenient punishment as they or the most part of them shall think fitt; alsoe our will and pleasure [is], concerning the judicial proceedings aforesaid, that the same shall be made and done summarily and verbally without writing until it come to the judgment or sentence, and yet, neverthelesse, our will and pleasure is that every judgment and sentence hereafter to be given in any of the causes aforesaid, or in any other of the said several Presidents and Councells or the greater number of them within their several limits and precincts, shall be breifely and summarily registred into a book to be kept for that purpose, together with the cause for which the said judgment or sentence was given; and that the said judgment and sentence soe registered and written shall be subscribed with the hands or names of the said President and Councel or such of them as gave the judgment or sentence; alsoe our will and pleasure is and wee doe hereby establish and ordaine that the said several Collonies and plantations, and every person and persons of the same, severally and respectively, shall within every of their several precincts for the space of five years next after their first landing upon the said coast of Virginia and America, trade together all in one stocke, or devideably but in two or three stocks att the most, and bring not only all the fruits of their labours there but alsoe all such other goods and commodities which shall be brought out of England or any other place into the same Collonies, into severall magazines or storehouses for that purpose to be made and erected there, and that in such order, manner and form as the Councel of that Collony or the more part of them shall sett downe and direct; and our will and pleasure is and wee doe in like manner ordaine that in every of the said Collonies and plantations there shall be chosen three, elected yearely by the President and Councell of every of the said several Colonies and plantations or the more part of them: one person of the same Colony and plantation to be Treasurer or Cape-merchant of the same Colony and plantation to take the charge and mannage-inge of all such goods, wares and commodities which shall be brought into or taken out of the several magazines or storehouses, the same Treasurer or Cape-merchant to continue in his office by the space of one whole year next after his said election, unless he shall happen to dye within the said year or voluntarily give over the same or be removed for any just or reasonalbe cause; and that thereupon the same President and Councell or the most part of them shall have power and authority to elect him again or any other or others in his room or stead to continue in the same office as aforesaid; and that alsoe there shall be two or more persons of good discretion within every of the said Colonies and plantations elected and chosen yearely, during the said terme of five years, by the President and Councel of the same Collony or the most part of them respectively within their several limits and precincts, the one or more of them to keep a book in which shall be registred and entred all such goods, wares and merchandizes as shall be received into the several magazines or storehouses within that Colony, being appointed for that purpose, and the other to keep a like book wherein shall be registred all goods, wares and merchandizes which shall issue or be taken out of any the several magazines or storehouses of that Collony, which clarks shall continue in their said places but att the will of the President and Councel of that Colony whereof he is, or of the major part of them; and that every person of every the said several Colonies and plantations shall be furnished with all necessaries out of those several magazines or storehouses which shall belong to the said Colony and plantation in which that person is, for and during the terme and time of five yeares by the appointment, direction and order of the President and Councell there, or of the said Cape-merchant and two clerks or of the most part of them within the said several limits and precincts of the said Colonies and plantations; alsoe our will and pleasure is and wee doe hereby ordain that the adventurers of the said First Colony and plantation shall and may during the said terme of five years elect and choose out of themselves one or more Companies, each Company consisting of three persons att the least who shall be resident att or neer London, or such other place and places as the Councel of the Colony for the time being, or the most part of them, during the said five years shall think fitt, who shall there from time to time take charge of the trade and accompt of all such goods, wares, merchandizes and other things which shall be sent from thence to the Company of the same Colony or plantation in Virginia, and likewise of all such wares, goods and merchandizes as shall be brought from the said Colony or plantation unto that place within our realme of England, and of all things concerning the mannaging of the affaires and profits concerning the adventurors of that Company which shall soe passe out of or come into that place or port; and likewise our will and pleasure is that the adventurors in the said Second Colony and plantation shall and may, during the said terme of five years, elect out of themselves one or more Companies, each Company consisting of three persons att the least who shall be resident att or near Plymouth in our county of Devon within our realme of England, and att such one, two or three other places or ports as the Councel of that Colony or the most part of them shall think fitt, who shall there from time to time take care and charge of the trade & accompt of all such goods, wares, merchandizes and other things which shall be sent from thence to the same Colony and plantation in Virginia, and likewise of all such goods, wares and merchandizes as shall be brought from the said Colony and plantation in Virginia into our realme of England, and of all things concerning the mannaging of the affaires and profits of the adventurors of that Company; alsoe our will and pleasure is that noe person or persons shall be admitted into any of the said Colonies and plantations, there to abide and remaine, but such as shall take not only the usual oath of obedience to us, our heires and successors; but alsoe the oath which is limitted in the last session of Parliament, holden at Westminster in the fourth year of our raigne, for their due obedience unto us, our heires and successors, that the trade to and from any the Colonies aforesaid may be mannaged to and from such ports & places within our realme of England as is before in these articles intended, any thing set down heretofore to the contrary notwithstanding; and that the said President and Councel of each of the said Colonies, and the more part of them respectively, shall and may lawfully from time to time constitute, make and ordaine such constitutions, ordinances and officers for the better order, government and peace of the people of their several Collonies, soe alwaies as the same ordinances and constitutions doe not touch any party in life or member, which constitutions & ordinances shall stand and continue in full force untill the same shall be otherwise altered or made void by us, our heires or successors, or our or their Councel of Virginia, soe alwaies as the same alterations be such as may stand with and be in substance consonant unto the lawes of England or the equity thereof; furthermore, our will and pleasure is and wee doe hereby determine and ordaine that every person and persons being our subjects of every the said Collonies and plantations shall from time to time well entreate those salvages in those parts and use all good meanes to draw the salvages and heathen people of the same several places and of the territories and countries adjoining to the true service and knowledge of God, and that all just, kind and charitable courses shall be holden with such of them as shall conforme themselves to any good and sociable traffique and dealing with the subjects of us, our heires and successors which shall be planted there, whereby they may be the sooner drawne to the true knowledge of God and the obedience of us, our heires and successors under such severe paines and punishments as shal be inflicted by the same several Presidents and Councells of the said several Colonies, or the most part of them, within their several limits and precincts, on such as shall offend therein or doe the contrary; and that as the said territories and countries of Virginia and America within the degrees aforesaid shall from time to time increase in plantation by our subjects, wee, our heires and successors will, ordaine and give such order and further instructions, lawes, constitutions and ordinances for the better rule, order and government of such as soe shall make plantations there as to us, our heires and successors shall from time to time be thought fitt & convenient, which alwaies shall be such as may stand with or be in substance consonant unto the lawes of England or the equity thereof; and lastly wee doe ordaine and establish for us, our heires and successors that such oath shall be taken by each of our Councellors here for Virginia, concerning their place and office of Councell, as by the Privy Councell of us, our heires and successors of this our realme of England shall be in that behalf limited & appointed; and that each Councellor of the said Colonies shall take such oath for the execution of their place and office of Councel as by the Councel of us, our heires and successors here in England, for Virginia, shall in that behalfe be limited and appointed; and aswell those several articles and instructions herein mentioned and contained as alsoe all such as by virtue hereof shall hereafter be made and ordained, shall as need shall require, by the advice of our Councel here for Virginia be transcripted over unto the said several Councells of the said several Colonies under the seale to be ordained for our said Councell here for Virginia; In witnesses &c.

Virginia State Library, "Patents, No. 2, 1643-1651"; Hening, Vol. I, pp. 67-75.

ORDINANCE AND CONSTITUTION

March 9, 1607

An ordinance and constitution enlarging the number of our Councel for the two several Colonies and plantations in Virginia and America between 34 and 45 degrees of northerly latitude, and augmenting their authority for the better directing and ordering of such things as shall concerne the said Colonies.

James, by the grace of God, &c. Whereas wee, by our letters patents under our Great Seale of England bearing date the tenth day of April last past, have given licence to sundry our loving subjects named in the said letters patents and to their associates to deduce and conduct two several Colonies or plantations of sundry our loving people willing to abide and inhabit in certaine parts of Virginia and America with divers preheminences, priviledges, authorities and other things, as in and by the said letters patents more particularly it appeareth; and whereas wee, according to the effect and true meaning of the said letters patents, have by a former instrument, signed with our hand and signe manuel and sealed with our Privy Seal of our realme of England, established and ordained that our trusty and welbeloved Sir William Wade, Knight, our Lieutenant of our Tower of London; Sir Thomas Smith, Knight; Sir Walter Cope, Knight; Sir George Moor, Knight; Sir Francis Popeham, Knight; Sir Ferdinando Gorges, Knight; Sir John Trevor, Knight; Sir Henry Montague, Knight, Recorder of our citty of London; Sir William Rumney, Knight; John Dodderidge, Esqr., our Solicitor General; Thomas Warr, Esq.; John Eldred, of our city of London, merchant; Thomas James, of our citty of Bristol, merchant; and James Bagge, of Plymouth in our county of Devon, merchant; should be our Councel for all matters which should happen in Virginia or any the territories of America aforesaid, or any actions, businesse or causes for and concerning the same, which Councel is from time to time to be encreased, altered or changed att the nomination of us, our heires and successors, and att our and their will and pleasure; & whereas our said Councel have found by experience their number being but fourteen in all and most of them dispersed by reason of their several habitations far and remote the one from the other, and many of them in like manner far remote from our citty of London where, if need require, they may receive directions from us and our Privy Councel and from whence instructions and directions may be by them left and more readily given for the said Colonies; that when very needful occasion requireth there cannot be any competent number of them by any meanes be drawne together for consultation; for remedy whereof our said loving subjects of the several Colonies aforesaid have been humble suitors unto us and have to that purpose offered to our Royal consideration the names of certaine sage and discreet persons, & having with like humility entreated us that the said persons, or soe many of them as to us should seem good, might be added unto them and might (during our pleasure) be of our Councel for the foresaid Colonies of Virginia; wee therefore for the better establishing, disposing, orderring and directing of the said several Colonies within the degrees aforesaid, and of all such affaires, matters and things as shall touch and concerne the same, doe, by these presents signed with our hand and signe manuel and sealed with our Privy Seale of our realme of England, establish and ordaine that our trusty and welbeloved Sir Thomas Challonor, Knight; Sir Henry Nevil, Knight; Sir Fulks Grevil, Knight; Sir John Scot, Knight; Sir Robert Mansfield, Knight; Sir Oliver Cromwel, Knight; Sir Morrice Berkeley, Knight; Sir Edward Michelbourne, Knight; Sir Thomas Holcroft, Knight; Sir Thomas Smith, Knight, Clerk of our Privy Councel; Sir Robert Kelligrew, Knight; Sir Robert Croft, Knight; Sir George Copping, Knight; Sir Edwyn Sandys, Knight; Sir Thomas Row, Knight; and Sir Anthony Palmer, Knight; nominated unto us by and on the behalfe of the said First Colony;

Sir Edward Hungerford, Knight; Sir John Mallet, Knight; Sir John Gilbert, Knight; Sir Thomas Freale, Knight; Sir Richard Hawkings, Knight; Sir Bartholomew Mitchel, Knight; Edward Seamour, Esq.; Bernard Greenville, Esq.; Edward Rogers, Esq.; and Matthew Sutcliffe, Doctor of Divinity; nominated to us by and on the behalfe of the said Second Colony, shall together with the persons formerly named, be our Councel for all matters which shall or may conduct to the aforesaid plantations or which shall happen in Virginia or any the territories of America between 34 & 45 degrees of northerly latitude from the aequinoctial line and the islands to the several Colonies limited and assigned, that is to say, the First Colony from 34 to 41 degrees of the said latitude, and the Second Colony between 38 and 45 degrees of the said latitude. And our further will and pleasure is, and by these presents for us, our heires and successors wee doe grant unto our said Councel of Virginia, that they or any twelve of them att the least, for the time being, whereof six att the least to be members of one of the said Colonies, and six more att the least to be members of the other Colony, shall have full power and authority to ordaine, nominate, elect and choose any other person or persons att their discretion to be and to serve as officer or officers to all offices and places that shall by them be thought fitt and requisite for the businesse and affaires of our said Councel and concerning the plantation or plantations aforesaid, and for the summoning, calling and assembling of the said Councel together when need shall require, or for summoning and calling before the said Councel any of the adventurors or others which shall passe on unto the said several Colonies to inhabit or to traffick there, or any other such like officer or officers which in time shall or may be found of use, behoofe or importance unto the Councel aforesaid. [And the said Council or any twelve of them as is aforesaid shall have full power and authority from time to time to continue or to alter or change the said officers and to elect and appoint others in their roomes and places, to make and ordain acts and ordinances for the better ordering, disposing and marshalling of the said several Colonies and the several adventurers or persons going to inhabit in the same several Colonies, or of any provision or provisions for the same, or for the direction of the officers aforesaid, or for the making of them to be subordinate or under jurisdiction one of another, and to do and execute all and every of their act and things which by any our grants or letters patents heretofore made they are warranted or authorised to do or execute so as always none of the said acts and ordinances or other things be contrary or repugnant to the true intent and meaning of our said letters patents granted for the plantation of the said several Colonies in Virginia and territories of America as aforesaid, or contrary to the laws and statutes in this our realm of England, or in derogation of our prerogative royal. Witness ourself at Westminster the ninth day of March (1607) in the year of our reign of England, France and Ireland the fourth, and of Scotland the fortieth, &c.][4]

Virginia State Library, "Patents, No. 2, 1643-1651"; Hening, Vol. I, pp. 76-79.

---

[4]Bracketed passage supplied from text in Hening.

THE SECOND CHARTER

May 23, 1609

James, by the grace of God [King of England, Scotland, France and Ireland, defender of the faith, etc.] To all [to whom these presents shall come, greeting.]

Whereas, at the humble suite and request of sondrie oure lovinge and well disposed subjects intendinge to deduce a colonie and to make habitacion and plantacion of sondrie of oure people in that parte of America comonlie called Virginia, and other part and territories in America either apperteyninge unto us or which are not actually possessed of anie Christian prince or people within certaine bound and regions, wee have formerly, by oure lettres patents bearinge date the tenth of Aprill in the fourth yeare of oure raigne of England, Fraunce, and Ireland, and the nine and thirtieth of Scotland, graunted to Sir Thomas Gates, Sir George Somers and others, for the more speedie accomplishment of the said plantacion and habitacion, that they shoulde devide themselves into twoe collonies—the one consistinge of divers Knights, gentlemen, merchaunts and others of our cittie of London, called the First Collonie; and the other of sondrie Knights, gentlemen and others of the citties of Bristoll, Exeter, the towne of Plymouth, and other places, called the Seccond Collonie—and have yielded and graunted maine and sondrie priviledges and liberties to each Collonie for their quiet setlinge and good government therein, as by the said lettres patents more at large appeareth.

Nowe, forasmuch as divers and sondrie of oure lovinge subjects, as well adventurers as planters, of the said First Collonie (which have alreadie engaged them selves in furtheringe the businesse of the said plantacion and doe further intende by the assistance of Almightie God to prosecute the same to a happie ende) have of late ben humble suiters unto us that, in respect of their great chardeges and the adventure of manie of their lives which they have hazarded in the said discoverie and plantacion of the said countrie, wee woulde be pleased to graunt them a further enlargement and explanacion of the said graunte, priviledge and liberties, and that suche counsellors and other officers maie be appointed amonngest them to manage and direct their affaires [as] are willinge and readie to adventure with them; as also whose dwellings are not so farr remote from the cittye of London but that they maie at convenient tymes be readie at hande to give advice and assistance upon all occacions requisite.

We, greatlie affectinge the effectual prosecucion and happie successe of the said plantacion and comendinge their good desires theirin, for their further encouragement in accomplishinge so excellent a worke, much pleasinge to God and profitable to oure Kingdomes, doe, of oure speciall grace and certeine knowledge and meere motion, for us, oure heires and successors, give, graunt and confirme to oure trustie and welbeloved subjects,

Robert, Earle of Salisburie [Salisbury]*
Thomas, Earle of Suffolke [Suffolk]
Henrie, Earle of Southampton
William, Earle of Pembroke
[Henrie], Earle of Lincolne [Lincoln]
Henrie, Earle of Dorsett [Dorset]
Thomas, Earle of Exeter
Phillipp, Earle of Mountgommery
Robert, Lord Vicount Lisle
Theophilus, Lord Howard of Walden
James Mountague, Lord Bishopp of Bathe and Wells
Edward, Lord Zouche
Thomas, Lord Lawarr
Wiliam, Lord Mounteagle
Raphe, Lord Ewre
Edmond, Lord Sheffeild [Sheffield]
Grey, Lord Shandis [Chandois]
[Grey], Lord Compton
John, Lord Petre
John, Lord Stanhope
George, Lord Carew
Sir Humfrey Welde, Lord Mayor of London [Weld]

*All names in brackets supplied from text in Stith.

George Pertie, Esquire
[Percie]
Sir Edward Cecill, Knight
[Cecil]
Sir George Wharton, Knight
Frauncis West, Esquire
Sir William Waade, Knight
[Wade]
Sir Henrie Nevill, Knight
[Nevil]
Sir Thomas Smithe, Knight
[Smith]
Sir Oliver Cromwell, Knight
Sir Peter Manwood, Knight
Sir Dru Drurie, Knight
[Drury]
Sir John Scott, Knight
[Scot]
Sir Thomas Challouer, Knight
[Challoner]
Sir Robert Drurie, Knight
[Drury]
Sir Anthonye Cope, Knight
Sir Horatio Veere, Knight
[Vere]
Sir Edward Conwaie, Knight
[Conway]
Sir William Browne
[Brown]
Sir Maurice Barkeley, Knight
[Berkeley]
Sir Roberte Maunsell, Knight
[Mansel]
Sir Amias Presou, Knight
[Preston]
Sir Thomas Gates, Knight
Sir Anthonie Ashley, Knight
[Ashly]
Sir Michaell Sandes, Knight
[Sandys]
Sir Henrie Carew, Knight
[Carey]
Sir Stephen Soame, Knight
Sir Calisthenes Brooke, Knight
Sir Edward Michelborne, Knight [Michelborn]
Sir John Racliffe, Knight
[Ratcliffe]
Sir Charles Willmott, Knight
[Wilmot]
Sir George Moore, Knight
[Moor]
Sir Hugh Wirrall, Knight
[Wirral]
Sir Thomas Dennys, Knight
[Dennis]
Sir John Hollis, Knight
[Holles]
Sir William Godolphin, Knight
Sir Thomas Monnson, Knight
[Monson]
Sir Thomas Ridgwaie, Knight
[Ridgwine]
Sir John Brooke, Knight
Sir Roberte Killigrew, Knight
Sir Henrie Peyton, Knight
Sir Richard Williamson, Knight
Sir Ferdinando Weynman, Knight
Sir William St. John, Knight
Sir Thomas Holcrofte, Knight
[Holcroft]
Sir John Mallory, Knight
Sir Roger Ashton, Knight
Sir Walter Cope, Knight
Sir Richard Wigmore, Knight
Sir William Cooke, Knight
[Coke]
Sir Herberte Crofte, Knight

Sir Henrie Faushawe, Knight [Fanshaw]
Sir John Smith, Knight
Sir Francis Wolley, Knight
Sir Edward Waterhouse, Knight
Sir Henrie Sekeford, Knight [Seekford]
Sir Edward Saudes, Knight[6] [Edwin Sandys]
Sir Thomas Wayneman, Knight [Waynam]
Sir John Trevor, Knight
Sir Warrwick Heale, Knight [Heele]
Sir Robert Wroth, Knight
Sir John Townnesende, Knight [Townsend]
Sir Christopher Perkins, Knight
Sir Daniell Dun, Knight
Sir Henrie Hobarte, Knight [Hobart]
Sir Franncis Bacon, Knight
Sir Henrie Mountague, Knight [Montague]
Sir Georg Coppin, Knight
Sir Samuell Sandes, Knight [Sandys]
Sir Thomas Roe, Knight
Sir George Somers, Knight
Sir Thomas Freake, Knight
Sir Thomas Horwell, Knight [Harwell]
Sir Charles Kelke, Knight
Sir Baptist Hucks, Knight [Hicks]
Sir John Watts, Knight
Sir Roberte Carey, Knight
Sir William Romney, Knight
Sir Thomas Middleton, Knight
Sir Hatton Cheeke, Knight
Sir John Ogle, Knighte
Sir Cavallero Meycot, Knight
Sir Stephen Riddlesden, Knight [Riddleson]
Sir Thomas Bludder, Knight
Sir Anthonie Aucher, Knight
Sir Robert Johnson, Knight
Sir Thomas Panton, Knight
Sir Charles Morgan, Knight
Sir Stephen Powle, Knight [Pole]
Sir John Burlacie, Knight
Sir Christofer Cleane, Knight [Cleave]
Sir George Hayward, Knight
Sir Thomas Dane, Knight [Davis]
Sir Thomas Dutton, Knight [Sutton]
Sir Anthonie Forrest, Knight [Forest]

[6]Stith's footnote: "The adventurers names are vastly confused and different in the different M. S. copies of this charter. I chose the two fairest and most correct copies, that I met with, to transcribe from; and altho' they both agree in writing this name, Sir *Edward Sands*, or *Sandis*, yet they are both certainly wrong, as might be easily proved, were it worth while, and would not be too tedious. I was also much puzzled to adjust and set right others of the names; and altho' I was at no small pains in collating the copies, and in consulting and referring to other ancient letters patents and papers, yet I will not affirm that I am not often mistaken. But however erroneous and perplexed the names of the adventurers may be, yet I found the main body, and material parts of the charter, very clear, full, and correct."

Sir Robert Payne, Knight
Sir John Digby, Knight
Sir Dudley Diggs, Knight [Digges]
Sir Rowland Cotton, Knight
Doctour Mathewe Rutcliffe [Sutcliffe]
Doctor Meddowes [Meadows]
Doctor Turner
Doctor Poe
Captaine Pagnam
Captaine Jeffrey Holcrofte
Captaine Raunne [Romney]
Captaine Henrie Spry
Captaine Shelpton [Shelton]
Captaine Spark [Sparks]
[Captain] Thomas Wyatt [Wyat]
Captaine Brinsley
Captaine William Courtney
Captaine Herbert
Captaine Clarke
Captaine Dewhurst
Captaine John Blundell
Captaine Frier [Fryer]
Captaine Lewis Orwell
Captaine Edward Lloyd [Loyd]
Captaine Slingesby
Captaine Huntley [Hawley]
Captaine Orme
Captaine Woodhouse
Captaine Mason
Captaine Thomas Holcroft
Captaine John Cooke [Coke]
Captaine Hollis [Holles]
Captaine William Proude
Captaine Henrie Woodhouse
Captaine Richard Lindeley [Lindesey]
Captaine Dexter
Captaine William Winter
Captaine Herle [Pearse]
Captain John Bingham
Captaine Burray
Captaine Thomas Conwey [Conway]
Captaine Rookwood
Captaine William Lovelace
Captaine John Ashley
Captaine Thomas Wynne
Captaine Thomas Mewtis
Captaine Edward Harwood
Captaine Michaell Evered [Everard]
Captaine Connoth [Comock]
Captaine Miles [Mills]
Captaine Pigott [Pigot]
Captaine Edward Maria Wingfeild [Wingfield]
Captaine Christopher Newporte [Newport]
Captaine John Siclemore, alias Ratcliffe [Sicklemore]
Captaine John Smith
Captyn John Martyn [Martin]

Captaine Peter Wynne
Captaine Waldoe
[Waldo]
Captyn Thomas Wood
Captaine Thomas Button
George Bolls, Esquire, Sheriffe of London
William Crashawe, [Clerk], Bachelor of Divinite
William Seabright, Esquire
Christopher Brook, Esquire
John Bingley, Esquire
Thomas Watson, Esquire
Richard Percivall, Esquire
[Percival]
John Moore, Esquire
Hugh Brooker, Esquire
David Waterhouse, Esquire
[Woodhouse]
Anthonie Auther, Esquier
[Aucher]
Roberte Bowyer, Esquire
[Boyer]
Raphe Ewens, Esquire
Zacharie Jones, Esquire
George Calvert, Esquire
William Dobson, Esquire
Henry Reynold, Esquire
[Reynolds]
Thomas Walker, Esquire
Anthonie Barnars, Esquire
Thomas Sandes, Esquire
[Sandys]
Henrie Sand, Esquire
[Sandys]
Richard Sand
[Sandys]
Sonne of Sir Edwin Sandes
[Sandys]
William Oxenbridge, Esquire

John Moore, Esquire
Thomas Wilson, Esquire
John Bullocke, Esquire
[Bullock]
John Waller, [Esquire]
Thomas Webb
Jehughe Robinson
William Brewster
Robert Evelyn
Henrie Dabenie
[Danby]
Richard Hacklewte, minister
[Hackluit]
John Eldred, marchaunt
[Eldrid]
William Russell, marchaunt
John Merrick, marchaunt
Richard Bannester, merchant
[Banister]
Charles Anthonie, goldsmithe
[Anthony]
John Banck
[Banks]
William Evans
Richard Humble
Robert Chamberleyne, marchaunt [Richard Chamberlayne]
Thomas Barber, marchaunt
Richard Pevyrell, merchaunt
[Pomet]
John Fletcher, merchant
Thomas Nicholls, merchant
John Stoak, merchaunt
[Stoke]
Gabriell Archer
Franncis Covell
[Covel]
William Bouham
[Bonham]

Edward Harrison
John Wolstenholme
Nicholas Salter
Hugh Evans
William Barners
[Barnes]
Otho Mawdett
[Mawdet]
Richard Staper, marchant
John Elkin, marchaunt
William Cayse
[Coyse]
Thomas Perkin, cooper
Humfrey Ramell, cooper
[Humphrey James]
Henry Jackson
Roberte Shingleton
[Singleton]
Christopher Nicholls
John Harper
Abraham Chamberlaine
[Chamberlayne]
Thomas Shipton
Thomas Carpenter
Anthoine Crewe
[Crew]
George Holman
Robert Hill
Cleophas Smithe
[Smith]
Raphe Harrison
John Farmer
James Brearley
William Crosley
[Crosby]
Richard Cocks
[Cox]
John Gearinge
[Gearing]

Richard Strough, iremonnger
[Strongarm]
Thomas Langton
Griffith Hinton
Richard Ironside
Richard Deane
[Dean]
Richard Turner
William Leveson, mercer
[Lawson]
James Chatfeilde
[Chatfield]
Edward Allen
[Edward Allen Tedder]
Tedder Roberts[7]
Heldebrand Sprinson
[Robert Hildebrand Sprinson]
Arthur Mouse
John Gardener
[Gardiner]
James Russell
[Russel]
Richard Casewell
[Caswell]
Richard Evanns
[Evans]
John Hawkins
Richard Kerrill
[Kerril]
Richard Brooke
Mathewe Scrivener, gentleman
[Screvener]
William Stallendge, gentleman
[Stallenge]
Arthure Venn, gentleman
Saund Webb, gentleman
[Sandys Webbe]

[7]Omitted from Stith.

Michaell Phettiplace, gentleman
William Phetiplace, gentleman
[Phettiplace]
Ambrose Brusey, gentleman
[Prusey]
John Taverner, gentleman
George Pretty, gentleman
Peter Latham, gentleman
Thomas Monnford, gentleman
[Montford]
William Cautrell, gentleman
[Cantrel]
Richard Wiffine, gentleman
[Wiffin]
Raphe Mooreton, gentleman
[Moreton]
John Cornellis
[Cornelius]
Martyn Freeman
Raphe Freeman
Andreau Moore
Thomas White
Edward Perkin
Robert Offley
Thomas Whitley
George Pitt
[Pit]
Roberte Parkehurste
[Parkhurst]
Thomas Morris
Peter Vaulore
[Harloe]
Jeffrey Duppa
John Gilbert
William Hancock
Mathew Bromrigg
[Brown]
Francis Tirrell
[Tyrrel]
Randall Carter
Othowell Smithe
[Smith]
Thomas Honnyman
[Hamond]
Marten Bonde, haberdasher
[Bond]
Joan Mousloe
[John Moulsoe]
Roberte Johnson
William Younge
[Young]
John Woddall
[Woodal]
William Felgate
Humfrey Westwood
Richard Champion
Henrie Robinson
Franncis Mapes
William Sambatch
[Sambach]
Rauley Crashawe
[Ralegh Crashaw]
Daniell Tucker
Thomas Grave
Hugh Willestone
Thomas Culpepper, of Wigsell, Esquire
John Culpepper, gentleman
Henrie Lee
Josias Kirton, gentleman
[Kerton]
John Porie, gentleman
[Pory]
Henrie Collins
George Burton
William Atkinson
Thomas Forrest
[Forest]

John Russell
[Russel]
John Houlte
[Holt]
Harman Harrison
Gabriell Beedell
[Beedel]
John Beedell
[Beedel]
Henrie Dankes
[Dawkes]
George Scott
[Scot]
Edward Fleetewood, gentleman
[Fleetwood]
Richard Rogers, gentleman
Arthure Robinson
Robert Robinson
John Huntley
John Grey
[Gray]
William Payne
William Feilde
[Field]
William Wattey
William Webster
John Dingley
Thomas Draper
Richard Glanvile
[Glanvil]
Arnolde Lulls
[Hulls]
Henrie Rowe
[Roe]
William Moore
[More]
Nicholas Grice
[Gryce]
James Monnger
[Monger]

Nicholas Andrewes
[Andrews]
Jerome Haydon, iremonnger
[Jeremy Haydon]
Phillipp Durrant
[Philip Durette]
John Quales
[Quarles]
John West
Mathew Springeham
[Springham]
John Johnson
Christopher Hore
George Barkeley
Thomas Sued
[Snead]
George Barkeley
[Berkeley]
Arthure Pett [Pet]
Thomas Careles
William Barkley
[Berkley]
Thomas Johnson
Alexander Bent
[Bents]
Captaine William Kinge
[King]
George Sandes, gentleman
[Sandys]
James White, gentleman
Edmond Wynn
[Wynne]
Charles Towler
Richard Reynold
Edward Webb
Richard Maplesden
Thomas Levers
[Lever]
David Bourne
Thomas Wood

Raphe Hamer
Edward Barnes, mercer
John Wright, mercer
Robert Middleton
Edward Litsfeild
[Littlefield]
Katherine West
Thomas Webb
[Web]
Raphe Kinge
[King]
Roberte Coppine
[Coppin]
James Askewe
Christopher Nicholls
[Christopher Holt]
William Bardwell
Alexander Childe
[Chiles]
Lewes Tate
Edward Ditchfeilde
[Ditchfield]
James Swifte
Richard Widdowes, goldesmith
Edmonde Brundell[8]
[Brudenell]
John Hanford
[Hansford]
Edward Wooller
William Palmer, haberdasher
John Badger
John Hodgson
Peter Monnsill
[Mounsel]
John Carrill
[Carril]
John Busbridge
[Bushridge]
William Dunn
[Dun]
Thomas Johnson
Nicholas Benson
Thomas Shipton
Nathaniell Wade
Randoll Wettwood
[Wetwood]
Mathew Dequester
Charles Hawkins
Hugh Hamersley
Abraham Cartwright
George Bennett
[Bennet]
William Cattor
[Cater]
Richard Goddart
Henrie Cromwell
Phinees Pett
[Pet]
Roberte Cooper[9]
Henrie Neite
[Newce]
Edward Wilks
[Wilkes]
Roberte Bateman
Nicholas Farrar
John Newhouse
John Cason
Thomas Harris, gentleman
George Etheridge, gentleman
Thomas Mayle, gentleman
Richard Stratford
[Stafford]
Thomas
Richard Cooper
John Westrowe
[Westrow]

[8]Between this name and that following Stith adds: "Edward Burwell."
[9]Between this name and that following Stith adds: "John Cooper."

Edward Welshe
[Welch]
Thomas Brittanie
[Britain]
Thomas Knowls
[Knowles]
Octavian Thorne
Edmonde Smyth
[Smith]
John March
Edward Carew
Thomas Pleydall
Richard Lea
[Let]
Miles Palmer
Henrie Price
John Josua, gentleman
[Joshua]
William Clawday
[Clauday]
Jerome Pearsye
John Bree, gentleman
William Hampson
Christopher Pickford
Thomas Hunt
Thomas Truston
Christopher Lanman
[Salmon]
John Haward, clerke
[Howard]
Richarde Partridge
Allen Cotton
[Cassen]
Felix Wilson
Thomas Colethurst
[Bathurst]
George Wilmer
Andrew Wilmer
Morrice Lewellin

Thomas Jedwin
[Godwin]
Peter Burgoyne
Thomas Burgoyne
Roberte Burgoyne
Roberte Smithe, merchauntay-
lor [Smith]
Edward Cage, grocer
Thomas Canon, gentleman
[Cannon]
William Welby, stacioner
Clement Wilmer, gentleman
John Clapham, gentleman
Giles Fraunces, gentleman
[Francis]
George Walker, sadler
John Swinehowe, stacioner
[Swinhow]
Edward Bushoppe, stacioner
[Bishop]
Leonard White, gentleman
Christopher Barron
[Baron]
Peter Benson
Richard Smyth
[Smith]
George Prockter, minister
[Proctor]
Millicent Ramesden, widowe
[Ramsdent]
Joseph Soane
Thomas Hinshawe
[Hinshaw]
John Baker
Robert Thorneton
[Thornton]
John Davies
[Davis]
Edward Facett
[Facet]

George Nuce, gentleman [Newce]
John Robinson
Captaine Thomas Wood
William Browne, shoemaker [Brown]
Roberte Barker, shoemaker
Roberte Penington [Pennington]
Francis Burley, minister
William Quick, grocer
Edward Lewes, grocer [Lewis]
Laurence Campe, draper
Aden Perkins, grocer
Richard Shepparde, preacher [Shepherd]
William Sheckley, haberdasher [Sherley]
William Tayler, haberdasher [Taylor]
Edward Lukyn, gentleman [Edwin Lukin]
John Francklyn, haberdasher [Franklyn]
John Southicke [Southwick]
Peter Peate
George Johan, iremonnger
George Yardley, gentleman [Yeardley]
Henrie Shelly [Shelley]
John Pratt [Prat]
Thomas Church, draper
William Powell, gentleman [Powel]
Richard Frithe, gentleman [Frith]
Thomas Wheeler, draper
Franncis Hasilerigg, gentleman [Haselrig]
Hughe Shippley, gentleman [Shipley]
John Andrewes, thelder, [doctor], of Cambridge [Andrews]
Franncis Whistley, gentleman [Whistler]
John Vassall, gentleman
Richard Howle
Edward Barkeley, gentleman [Berkeley]
Richard Knerisborough, gentleman [Keneridgburg]
Nicholas Exton, draper
William Bennett, fishmonger [Bennet]
James Hawood, marchaunt [Haywood]
Nicholas Isaak, merchaunt [Isaac]
William Gibbs, merchannt
[William] Bushopp [Bishop]
Barnard Michell [Mitchel]
Isaake Michell [Isaac Mitchel]
John Streat [Streate]
Edward Gall
John Marten, gentleman [Martin]
Thomas Fox
Luke Lodge
John Woodleefe, gentleman [Woodliffe]

Rice Webb
[Richard]
Vincent Lowe
[Low]
Samuell Burnam
[Burnham]
Edmonde Pears, haberdasher
Josua Goudge
[John Googe]
John St. John
Edwarde Vaughan
William Dunn
Thomas Alcock
[Alcocke]
John Andrewes, the younger, of Cambridge [Andrews]
Samuell Smithe
[Smith]
Thomas Jerrard
[Gerrard]
Thomas Whittingham
William Cannynge
[Canning]
Paule Caminge
[Canning]
George Chaudler
[Chandler]
Henrye Vincent
Thomas Ketley
James Skelton
James Montain
[Mountaine]
George Webb, gentleman
Josephe Newbroughesmith
[Joseph Newbridge, smith]
Josias Mande
[Mand]
Raphe Haman, the younger
[Hamer]
Edward Brewster, the sonne of William Brewster
Leonard Harwood, mercer
Phillipp Druerdent
William Carpenter
Tristram Hill
Roberte Cock, grocer
Laurence Grene, grocer
[Greene]
Daniell Winche, grocer
[Samuel Winch]
Humfrey Stile, grocer
Averie Dransfeild, grocer
[Dransfield]
Edwarde Hodges, grocer
Edward Beale, grocer[10]
Raphe Busby, grocer[11]
John Whittingham, grocer
John Hide, grocer
Mathew Shipperd, grocer
[Shepherd]
Thomas Allen, grocer
Richard Hooker, grocer
Laurence Munckas, grocer
[Munks]
John Tanner, grocer
Peter Gate, grocer
John Blunt, grocer[12]
Roberte Berrisford, grocer[13]
Thomas Wells, gentleman[14]
John Ellis, grocer

[10]Between this name and that following Stith adds: "Thomas Culler, grocer."
[11]Name given twice in P. R. O. transcript.
[12]Between this name and that following Stith adds: "Robert Phips, grocer."
[13]Name given twice in P. R. O. transcript.
[14]Stith reads: "Thomas Wells, grocer."

Henrie Colthurst, grocer
John Cranage, grocer
[Cavady]
Thomas Jenings, grocer
[Jennings]
Edmond Peshall, grocer
[Pashall]
Timothie Bathurst, grocer
Gyles Parslowe, grocer[15]
[Parslow]
Roberte Johnson, grocer
[Richard]
William Janson, vintener
[Johnson]
Ezechiell Smith
Richard Murrettone
[Martin]
William Sharpe
Roberte Ritche
[Rich]
William Stannerd, inholder
[Stannard]
John Stocken
William Strachey, gentleman
George Farmer, gentleman
Thomas Gypes, clothworker
Abraham Dawes, gentleman
[Davies]
Thomas Brockett, gentleman
[Brocket]
George Bathe, fishmonger
[Bache]
John Dike, fishmonger
Henrie Spranger
Richard Farringdon
[Farrington]
Chistopher Vertue, vintener
Thomas Baley, vintener
[Bayley]
George Robins, vintener
Tobias Hinson, grocer
Urian Spencer
[Vrian]
Clement Chachelley
[Chicheley]
John Searpe, gentleman
[Scarpe]
James Cambell, iremonnger
[Campbell]
Christopher Clitherowe, iremonnger [Clitheroe]
Phillipp Jacobson
Peter Jacobson, of Andwarpe
William Barckley
[Berkeley]
Miles Banck, cutler
[Banks]
Peter Highley, grocer
[Higgons]
Henrie John, gentleman
John Stoakley, merchauntailor
[Stokeley]
The companie of mercers
The companie of grocers
The companie of drapers
The company of fishmongers
The companie of gouldsmithes
The companie of skynners
The companie merchauntailors
The companie of haberdashers
The companie of salters
The companie of iremongers
The companie of vintners
The companie of clothworkers
The companie of dyers
The companie of bruers
The companie of lethersellers
The companie of pewterers

[15]Between this name and that following Stith adds: "Robert Milmay, grocer."

The companie of cutlers
The companie of whitebakers
The companie of waxchaundlers
The companie of tallowe chaundlers
The companie of armorers
The companie of girdlers
The companie of butchers
The companie of sadlers
The companie of carpenters
The companie of cordwayners
The companie of barbor chirurgions
The companie of painter stayners
The companie of curriers
The companie of masons
The companie of plumbers
The companie of inholders
The companie of founders
The companie of poulterers
The companie of cookes
The companie of coopers
The companie of tylers and bricklayers
The companie of bowyers
The companie of fletchers
The companie of blacksmithes
The companie of joyners
The companie of weavers
The companie of wollmen
The companie of woodmonngers
The companie of scrivenors
The companie of fruterers
The companie of plasterers
The companie of brownebakers
The companie of stacioners
The companie of imbroderers
The companie of upholsters
The companie of musicions
The companie of turners[16]
The companie of baskettmakers
The companie of glasiers
John Levett, merchaunt [Levet]
Thomas Nornicott, clothworker [Nornicot]
Richard Venn, haberdasher
Thomas Scott, gentleman [Scot]
Thomas Juxson, merchauntaylor [Juxon]
George Hankinson
Thomas Leeyer, gentleman [Seyer]
Mathew Cooper
George Butler, gentleman
Thomas Lawson, gentleman
Edward Smith, haberdasher
Stephen Sparrowe
John Jones, merchaunt
[John] Reynold, brewer [Reynolds]
Thomas Plummer, merchaunt
James Duppa, bruer
Rowland Coytemore [Coitmore]
William Sotherne [Southerne]
George Whittmoore, haberdasher [Whitmore]
Anthonie Gosoulde, the younger [Gosnold]

[16]Following this Stith adds: "The Company of Gardiners."

John Allen, fishemonger
Symonde Yeomans, fishmonger [Simon]
Launcelot Davis, gentleman
John Hopkins, an alderman of Bristoll
John Kettlebye, gentleman [Kettleby]
Richard Chene, gouldsmithe [Clene]
George Hooker, gentleman
Roberte Shevinge, yeoman [Chening]

And to such and so manie as they doe or shall hereafter admitt to be joyned with them, in forme hereafter in theis presentes expressed, whether they goe in their persons to be planters there in the said plantacion, or whether they goe not, but doe adventure their monyes, goods or chattels, that they shalbe one bodie or communaltie perpetuall and shall have perpetual succession and one common seale to serve for the saide bodie or communaltie; and that they and their successors shalbe knowne, called and incorporated by the name of The Tresorer and Companie of Adventurers and Planters of the Citty of London for the Firste Collonie in Virginia.

And that they and their successors shalbe from hensforth, forever enabled to take, acquire and purchase, by the name aforesaid (licens for the same from us, oure heires or successors first had and obtained) anie manner of lands, tenements and hereditaments, goods and chattels, within oure realme of England and dominion of Wales; and that they and their successors shalbe likewise enabled, by the name aforesaid, to pleade and to be impleaded before anie of oure judges or justices, in anie oure courts, and in anie accions or suits whatsoever.

And wee doe also, of oure said speciall grace, certaine knowledge and mere mocion, give, grannte and confirme unto the said Tresorer and Companie, and their successors, under the reservacions, limittacions and declaracions hereafter expressed, all those lands, countries and territories scituat, lieinge and beinge in that place of America called Virginia, from the pointe of lande called Cape or Pointe Comfort all alonge the seacoste to the northward twoe hundred miles and from the said pointe of Cape Comfort all alonge the sea coast to the southward twoe hundred miles; and all that space and circuit of lande lieinge from the sea coaste of the precinct aforesaid upp unto the lande, throughoute, from sea to sea, west and northwest; and also all the island beinge within one hundred miles alonge the coaste of bothe seas of the precincte aforesaid; togeather with all the soiles, groundes, havens and portes, mynes, aswell royall mynes of golde and silver as other mineralls, pearles and precious stones, quarries, woods, rivers, waters, fishings, comodities, jurisdictions, royalties, priviledges, franchisies and preheminences within the said territorie and the precincts there of whatsoever; and thereto or there abouts, both by sea and lande, beinge or in anie sorte belonginge or appertayninge, and which wee by oure lettres patents maie or cann graunte; and in as ample manner and sorte as wee or anie oure noble progenitors have heretofore graunted to anie companie, bodie pollitique or corporate, or to anie adventurer or adventurers, undertaker or undertakers, of anie discoveries, plantacions or traffique of, in, or into anie forraine parts whatsoever; and in as large and ample manner as if the same were herin particulerly mentioned and expressed: to have, houlde, possesse and enjoye all and singuler the said landes, countries and territories with all and singuler other the premisses heretofore by theis [presents] graunted or mencioned to be grannted, to them, the said Tresorer and Companie, their successors and assignes, forever; to the sole and proper use of them, the said Tresorer and Companie, their successors and assignes [forever], to be holden of us, oure heires and successors, as of oure mannour of Estgreenewich, in free and common socage and not in capite; yeldinge and payinge, therefore, to us, oure heires and successors, the fifte parte onlie of all oare of gould and silver that from tyme to time, and at all times hereafter, shalbe there gotton, had and obtained, for all manner of service.

And, nevertheles, oure will and pleasure is, and wee doe by

theis presentes chardge, commannde, warrant and auctorize, that the said Tresorer and Companie and their successors, or the major parte of them which shall be present and assembled for that purpose, shall from time to time under their common seale distribute, convey, assigne and set over such particuler porcions of lands, tenements and hereditaments, by theise presents formerly grannted, unto such oure lovinge subjects naturallie borne of denizens, or others, aswell adventurers as planters, as by the said Companie, upon a commission of survey and distribucion executed and retourned for that purpose, shalbe named, appointed and allowed, wherein oure will and pleasure is, that respect be had as well of the proporcion of the adventure[r] as to the speciall service, hazarde, exploite or meritt of anie person so as to be recompenced, advannced or rewarded.

And for as muche as the good and prosperous successe of the said plantacion cannot but cheiflie depende, next under the blessinge of God and the supporte of oure royall aucthoritie, upon the provident and good direccion of the whole enterprise by a carefull and understandinge Counsell, and that it is not convenient that all the adventurers shalbe so often drawne to meete and assemble as shalbe requisite for them to have metings and conference aboute theire affaires, therefore we doe ordaine, establishe and confirme that there shalbe perpetually one Counsell here resident, accordinge to the tenor of oure former lettres patents, which Counsell shall have a seale for the better governement and administracion of the said plantacion besides the legall seale of the Companie or Corporacion, as in oure former lettres patents is also expressed.

And further wee establishe and ordaine that

Henrie, Earl of Southampton
William, Earl of Pembrooke
Henrie, Earl of Lincoln
Thomas, Earl of Exeter
Roberte, Lord Viscounte Lisle
Lord Theophilus Howard
James, Lord Bishopp of Bathe and Wells
Edward, Lord Zouche
Thomas, Lord Laware

William, Lord Mounteagle
Edmunde, Lord Sheffeilde
Grey, Lord Shanndoys [Chandois][17]
John, Lord Stanhope
George, Lord Carew
Sir Humfrey Welde, Lord Mayor of London
Sir Edward Cecil
Sir William Waad [Wade]
Sir Henrie Nevill
Sir Thomas Smith
Sir Oliver Cromwell
Sir Peter Manwood
Sir Thomas Challoner
Sir Henrie Hovarte [Hobart]
Sir Franncis Bacon
Sir George Coppin
Sir John Scott
Sir Henrie Carey
Sir Roberte Drurie [Drury]
Sir Horatio Vere
Sir Eward Conwaye [Conway]
Sir Maurice Berkeley [Barkeley]
Sir Thomas Gates
Sir Michaele Sands [Sandys]
Sir Roberte Mansfeild [Mansel]
Sir John Trevor
Sir Amyas Preston
Sir William Godolphin
Sir Walter Cope
Sir Robert Killigrewe
Sir Henrie Faushawe [Fanshaw]
Sir Edwyn Sandes [Sandys]
Sir John Watts
Sir Henrie Montague
Sir William Romney
Sir Thomas Roe
Sir Baptiste Hicks
Sir Richard Williamson
Sir Stephen Powle [Poole]
Sir Dudley Diggs
Christopher Brooke, [Esq.]
John Eldred, and
John Wolstenholme

shalbe oure Counsell for the said Companie of Adventurers and Planters in Virginia.

And the said Sir Thomas Smith wee ordaine to be Tresorer of the said Companie, which Tresorer shall have aucthoritie to give order for the warninge of the Counsell and sommoninge the Companie to their courts and meetings.

And the said Counsell and Tresorer or anie of them shalbe from henceforth nominated, chosen, contynued, displaced, chaunged, altered and supplied, as death or other severall oc-

[17]All names in brackets are taken from the text in Stith.

casions shall require, out of the Companie of the said adventurers by the voice of the greater parte of the said Counsell and adventurers in their assemblie for that purpose; provided alwaies that everie Councellor so newlie elected shalbe presented to the Lord Channcellor of England, or to the Lord Highe Treasurer of England, or the Lord Chambleyne of the housholde of us, oure heires and successors, for the tyme beinge to take his oathe of a Counsellor to us, oure heires and successors, for the said Companie and Collonie in Virginia.

And wee doe by theis presents, of oure especiall grace, certaine knowledge and meere motion, for us, oure heires and successors grannte unto the said Tresorer and Companie and their successors, that if it happen at anie time or times the Tresorer for the tyme beinge to be sick, or to have anie such cause of absente from the cittie of London as shalbe allowed by the said Counsell or the greater parte of them assembled, so as he cannot attende the affaires of that Companie, in everie such case it shall and maie be lawfull for such Tresorer for the tyme beinge to assigne, constitute and appointe one of the Counsell for Companie to be likewise allowed by the Counsell or the greater parte of them assembled to be the deputie Tresorer for the said Companie; which Deputie shall have power to doe and execute all things which belonge to the said Tresorer duringe such tyme as such Tresorer shalbe sick or otherwise absent, upon cause allowed of by the said Counsell or the major parte of them as aforesaid, so fullie and wholie and in as large and ample manner and forme and to all intents and purposes as the said Tresorer if he were present himselfe maie or might doe and execute the same.

And further of oure especiall grace, certaine knowledge and meere mocion, for us, oure heires and successors, wee doe by theis presents give and grannt full power and aucthoritie to oure said Counsell here resident aswell at this present tyme as hereafter, from time to time, to nominate, make, constitute, ordaine and confirme by such name or names, stile or stiles as to them shall seeme good, and likewise to revoke, dischardge, channge and alter aswell all and singuler governors, oficers and ministers which alreadie hath ben made, as also which hereafter shalbe by them thought fitt and meedefull to be made or used for the government of the said Colonie and plantacion.

And also to make, ordaine and establishe all manner of orders, lawes, directions, instructions, formes and ceremonies of government and magistracie, fitt and necessarie, for and concerninge the government of the said Colonie and plantacion; and the same att all tymes hereafter to abrogate, revoke or chaunge, not onely within the precincts of the said Colonie but also upon the seas in goeing and cominge to and from the said Collonie, as they in their good discrecions shall thinke to be fittest for [the] good of the adventurers and inhabiters there.

And we doe also declare that for divers reasons and consideracions us thereunto especiallie moving, oure will and pleasure is and wee doe hereby ordaine that imediatlie from and after such time as anie such governour or principall officer so to be nominated and appointed by oure said Counsell for the governement of the said Colonie, as aforesaid, shall arive in Virginia and give notice unto the Collonie there resident of oure pleasure in this behalfe, the government, power and aucthority of the President and Counsell, heretofore by oure former lettres patents there established, and all lawes and constitucions by them formerlie made, shall utterly cease and be determined; and all officers, governours and ministers formerly constituted or appointed shalbe dischardged, anie thinge in oure said former lettres patents conserninge the said plantacion contayned in aniewise to the contrarie notwithstandinge; streightlie chardginge and commaundinge the President and Counsell nowe resident in the said Collonie upon their alleadgiance after knowledge given unto them of oure will and pleasure by theis presentes signified and declared, that they forth with be obedient to such governor or governers as by oure said Counsell here resident shalbe named and appointed as aforesaid; and to all direccions, orders and commandements which they shall receive from them, aswell in the present resigninge and giveinge upp of their aucthoritie, offices, chardg and places, as in all other attendannce as shalbe by them from time to time required.

And wee doe further by theis presentes ordaine and establishe that the said Tresorer and Counsell here resident, and their successors or anie fower of them assembled (the Tresorer beinge one), shall from time to time have full power and aucthoritie to admitt and receive anie other person into their companie, corporacion and freedome; and further, in a generall assemblie of the adventurers, with the consent of the greater parte upon good cause, to disfranchise and putt oute anie person or persons oute of the said fredome and Companie.

And wee doe also grannt and confirme for us, oure heires and successors that it shalbe lawfull for the said Tresorer and Companie and their successors, by direccion of the Governors there, to digg and to serche for all manner of mynes of goulde, silver, copper, iron, leade, tinne and other mineralls aswell within the precincts aforesaid as within anie parte of the maine lande not formerly graunted to anie other; and to have and enjoye the gould, silver, copper, iron, leade, and tinn, and all other mineralls to be gotten thereby, to the use and behoofe of the said Companie of Planters and Adventurers, yeldinge therefore and payinge yerelie unto us, oure heires and successors, as aforesaid.

And wee doe further of oure speciall grace, certaine knowledge and meere motion, for us, oure heires and successors, grannt, by theis presents to and withe the said Tresorer and Companie and their successors, that it shalbe lawfull and free for them and their assignes at all and everie time and times here after, oute of oure realme of England and oute of all other [our] dominions, to take and leade into the said voyage, and for and towards the said plantacion, and to travell thitherwards and to abide and inhabite therein the said Colonie and plantacion, all such and so manie of oure lovinge subjects, or anie other straungers that wilbecomme oure lovinge subjects and live under oure allegiance, as shall willinglie accompanie them in the said voyadge and plantation with sufficient shippinge, armour, weapons, ordinannce, municion, powder, shott, victualls, and such merchaundize or wares as are esteemed by the wilde people in those parts, clothinge, implements, furnitures, catle, horses and mares, and all other thinges necessarie for the said plantation and for their use and defence and trade with the people there, and in passinge and retourninge to and from without yeldinge or payinge subsedie, custome, imposicion, or anie other taxe or duties to us, oure heires or successors, for the space of seaven yeares from the date of theis presents; provided, that none of the said persons be such as shalbe hereafter by speciall name restrained by us, oure heires or successors.

And for their further encouragement, of oure speciall grace and favour, wee doe by theis present for us, oure heires and successors, yeild and graunte to and with the said Tresorer and Companie and their successors and everie of them, their factors and assignes, that they and every of them shalbe free and quiett of all subsedies and customes in Virginia for the space of one and twentie yeres, and from all taxes and imposicions for ever, upon anie goods or merchaundizes at anie time or times hereafter, either upon importation thither or exportation from thence into oure realme of England or into anie other of oure [realms or] dominions, by the said Tresorer and Companie and their successors, their deputies, factors [or] assignes or anie of them, except onlie the five pound per centum due for custome upon all such good and merchaundizes as shalbe brought or imported into oure realme of England or anie other of theis oure dominions accordinge to the auncient trade of merchannts, which five poundes per centum onely beinge paid, it shalbe thensforth lawfull and free for the said Adventurers the same goods [and] merchaundizes to export and carrie oute of oure said dominions into forraine partes without anie custome, taxe or other duty to be paide to us, oure heires or successors or to anie other oure officers or deputies; provided, that the saide goods and merchaundizes be shipped out within thirteene monethes after their first landinge within anie parte of those dominions.

And wee doe also confirme and grannt to the said Tresorer and Companie, and their successors, as also to all and everie such governer or other officers and ministers as by oure said Counsell shalbe appointed, to have power and aucthoritie of governement and commannd in or over the said Colonie or plantacion; that they and everie of them shall and lawfullie maie from tyme to tyme and at all tymes forever hereafter, for their severall defence and safetie, enconnter, expulse, repell and resist by force and armes, aswell by sea as by land, and all waies and meanes whatsoever, all and everie such person and persons whatsoever as without the speciall licens of the said Tresorer and Companie and their successors shall attempte to inhabite within the said severall precincts and lymitts of the said Colonie and plantacion; and also, all and everie such person and persons whatsoever as shall enterprise, or attempte at anie time hereafter, destruccion, invasion, hurte, detriment or annoyannce to the said Collonye and plantacion, as is likewise specified in the said former grannte.

And that it shalbe lawful for the said Tresorer and Companie, and their successors and everie of them, from time to time and at all times hereafter, and they shall have full power and aucthoritie, to take and surprise by all waies and meanes whatsoever all and everie person and persons whatsoever, with their shippes, goods and other furniture, traffiquinge in anie harbor, creeke or place within the limitts or precincts of the said Colonie and plantacion, [not] beinge[18] allowed by the said Companie to be adventurers or planters of the said Colonie, untill such time as

[18]Stith's footnote: "It is *and being* in the original; but the sense carried me so clearly to it, that I ventured to make this correction, letting the reader at the same time know it."

they beinge of anie realmes or dominions under oure obedience shall paie or agree to paie, to the hands of the Tresorer or [of] some other officer deputed by the said governors in Virginia (over and above such subsedie and custome as the said Companie is or here after shalbe to paie) five poundes per centum upon all goods and merchaundizes soe brought in thither, and also five per centum upon all goods by them shipped oute from thence; and being straungers and not under oure obedience untill they have payed (over and above such subsedie and custome as the same Tresorer and Companie and their successors is or hereafter shalbe to paie) tenn pounds per centum upon all such goods, likewise carried in and oute, any thinge in the former lettres patents to the contrarie not withstandinge; and the same sommes of monie and benefitt as aforesaid for and duringe the space of one and twentie yeares shalbe wholie imploied to the benefitt and behoof of the said Colonie and plantacion; and after the saide one and twentie yeares ended, the same shalbe taken to the use of us, oure heires or successors, by such officer and minister as by us, oure heires or successors, shalbe thereunto assigned and appointed, as is specified in the said former lettres patents.

Also wee doe, for us, oure heires and successors, declare by theis presents, that all and everie the persons beinge oure subjects which shall goe and inhabit within the said Colonye and plantacion, and everie of their children and posteritie which shall happen to be borne within [any] the lymitts thereof, shall have [and] enjoye all liberties, franchesies and immunities of free denizens and naturall subjects within anie of oure other dominions to all intents and purposes as if they had bine abidinge and borne within this oure kingdome of England or in anie other of oure dominions.

And forasmuch as it shalbe necessarie for all such our lovinge subjects as shall inhabitt within the said precincts of Virginia aforesaid to determine to live togither in the feare and true woorshipp of Almighthie God, Christian peace and civill quietnes, each with other, whereby everie one maie with more safety, pleasure and profitt enjoye that where unto they shall attaine with great paine and perill, wee, for us, oure heires and successors, are likewise pleased and contented and by theis presents doe give and graunte unto the said Tresorer and Companie and their successors and to such governors, officers and ministers as shalbe, by oure said Councell, constituted and appointed, according to the natures and lymitts of their offices and places respectively, that they shall and maie from time to time for ever hereafter, within the said precincts of Virginia or in the waie by the seas thither and from thence, have full and absolute power and aucthority to correct, punishe, pardon, governe and rule all such the subjects of us, oure heires and successors as shall from time to time adventure themselves in anie voiadge thither or that shall at anie tyme hereafter inhabitt in the precincts and territorie of the said Colonie as aforesaid, accordinge to such order, ordinaunces, constitution, directions and instruccions as by oure said Counsell, as aforesaid, shalbe established; and in defect thereof, in case of necessitie according to the good discretions of the said governours and officers respectively, aswell in cases capitall and criminall as civill, both marine and other, so alwaies as the said statuts, ordinannces and proceedinges as neere as convenientlie maie be, be agreable to the lawes, statutes, government and pollicie of this oure realme of England.

And we doe further of oure speciall grace, certeine knowledge and mere mocion, grant, declare and ordaine that such principall governour as from time to time shall dulie and lawfullie be aucthorised and appointed, in manner and forme in theis presents heretofore expressed, shall [have] full power and aucthoritie to use and exercise marshall lawe in cases of rebellion or mutiny in as large and ample manner as oure leiutenant in oure counties within oure realme of England have or ought to have by force of their comissions of lieutenancy.

And furthermore, if anie person or persons, adventurers or planters, of the said Colonie, or anie other at anie time or times hereafter, shall transporte anie monyes, goods or marchaundizes oute of anie [of] oure kingdomes with a pretence or purpose to lande, sell or otherwise dispose the same within the lymitts and bounds of the said Collonie, and yet nevertheles beinge at sea or after he hath landed within anie part of the said Colonie shall carrie the same into anie other forraine Countrie, with a purpose there to sell and dispose there of that, then all the goods and chattels of the said person or persons so offendinge and transported, together with the shipp or vessell wherein such transportacion was made, shalbe forfeited to us, oure heires and successors.

And further, oure will and pleasure is, that in all questions and doubts that shall arrise upon anie difficultie of construccion or interpretacion of anie thinge contained either in this or in oure said former lettres patents, the same shalbe taken and interpreted in most ample and beneficiall manner for the said Tresorer and Companie and their successors and everie member there of.

And further, wee doe by theis presents ratifie and confirme unto the said Tresorer and Companie and their successors all privuleges, franchesies, liberties and immunties graunted in oure said former lettres patents and not in theis oure lettres patents revoked, altered, channged or abridged.

And finallie, oure will and pleasure is and wee doe further hereby for us, oure heires and successors grannte and agree, to and with the said Tresorer and Companie and their successors, that all and singuler person and persons which shall at anie time or times hereafter adventure anie somme or sommes of money in and towards the said plantacion of the said Colonie in Virginia and shalbe admitted by the said Counsell and Companie as adventurers of the said Colonie, in forme aforesaid, and shalbe enrolled in the booke or record of the adventurers of the said Companye, shall and maie be accompted, accepted taken, helde and reputed Adventurers of the said Collonie and shall and maie enjoye all and singuler grannts, priviledges, liberties, benefitts, profitts, commodities [and immunities], advantages and emoluments whatsoever as fullie, largely, amplie and absolutely as if they and everie of them had ben precisely, plainely, singulerly and distinctly named and inserted in theis oure lettres patents.

And lastely, because the principall effect which wee cann desier or expect of this action is the conversion and reduccion of the people in those partes unto the true worshipp of God and Christian religion, in which respect wee would be lothe that anie person should be permitted to passe that wee suspected to affect the superstitions of the Churche of Rome, wee doe hereby declare that it is oure will and pleasure that none be permitted to passe in anie voiadge from time to time to be made into the saide countrie but such as firste shall have taken the oath of supremacie, for which purpose wee doe by theise presents give full power and aucthoritie to the Tresorer for the time beinge, and anie three of the Counsell, to tender and exhibite the said oath to all such persons as shall at anie time be sent and imploied in the said voiadge.

Although expresse mention [of the true yearly value or certainty of the premises, or any of them, or of any other gifts or grants, by us or any of our progenitors or predecessors, to the aforesaid Treasurer and Company heretofore made, in these presents is not made; or any act, statute, ordinance, provision, proclamation, or restraint, to the contrary hereof had, made, ordained, or provided, or any other thing, cause, or matter, whatsoever, in any wise notwithstanding.] In witnes whereof [we have caused these our letters to be made patent. Witness ourself at Westminster, the 23d day of May (1609) in the seventh year of our reign of England, France, and Ireland, and of Scotland the ****]

Per ipsum Regem exactum.

P. R. O. Chancery Patent Rolls (c. 66), 1796, 5; Stith, Appendix, pp. 8-22; Hening, Vol. I, pp. 80-98.

VIRGINIA COUNCIL. "INSTRUCCIONS ORDERS AND CONSTITUCIONS . . . TO SR THOMAS GATES KNIGHT GOVERNOR OF VIRGINIA"

May, 1609

Instruccions, orders and constitucions by way of advise sett downe, declared and propounded to Sir Thomas Gates, Knight, Governor of Virginia and of the Colony there planted and to be planted, and of all the inhabitants thereof, by us His Majesties Counsell for the direction of the affaires of that countrey for his better disposinge and proceedinge in the government thereof accordinge to the authority and power given unto us by virtue of His Majesties lettres patents.

1. Havinge considered the greate sufficiency and zealous affeccion which you, Sir Thomas Gates, have many waies manifested unto us, and havinge therefore by our Commission under our hands and seales constituted and ordained you to be the Governor of Virginia, wee His Majesties Counsell for that plantacion, have consulted and advised uppon divers instruccions for your safer and more deliberate proceedinge therein; and therefore doe requier and charge you, accordinge to the Comission in that behalf directed unto you, presently with all convenient speede to take the charge and of our fleete consistinge of eight good shippes and one pinnace and of sixe hundred land men to be transported under your commaund, and with the first winde to sett saile for Virginia. And in your passage thither you shall not land nor touch any of the Kinge of Spaines his Dominions quetly possessed, without the leave or licence of the governor of such place as you shal by accident or contrary windes be forced into. You shall also hold counsell with the masters and pilotts and men of the best experience what way is safest and fittest for you to take, because we hold it daungerous that you should keepe the old

course of Dominico and Meins lest you fall into the hand of the Spaniard, who may attend in that roade ready to intercept you:

2. When it shall please God that you have safely attained the Kings River, and our porte and seate of James Towne in Virginia, wee advise you to call by proclamacion into some publique place, all the governors, officers, and other His Majesties subjects aswell already seated there as transported with you, to whom you shall cause your Commission to be directly reade, whereby signifi cacion may be had of His Majesties pleasure in establishinge you the Governor of that countrey and plantacion, and the President, Councell and Colony there may take notice of the revocacion of that fourme of governement by the first lettres patents constituted and confirmed, and accordingly yeald due obedience unto you, their Governor.

3. You shall demaund then and resume into your hands the former lettres pattents and all instruccions & publique instruments given or sent unto them and all bookes and records whatsoever of the generall proceedings untill this time, and dispose of them in the future accordinge to your discrecion.

4. Beinge setled in your government, you shall call unto you, for your further advise and graver proceedinge, their principall officers and gentlemen whom we do ordaine and appointe to be of the Councell and who for earliness of their undertakings and their greate paines and merits doe well deserve this honor & respect from us: Sir George Summers, Knight, and Admirall of Virginia; Captaine John Smith, nowe President; Captaine John Radclif; Captaine Peter Winne, Seirjant Major of the fort; Mr. Mathewe Scrivenor, whom out of our good experience of his abilities in that kinde we doe name and appointe to be Secretary of that Councell; Captaine John Martine; Captaine Richard Waldoe, master of the workes; Captaine Woode; and Mr. Fleetwoode, whom we assure ourselves you will use with all good respecte in their places and to whome wee expecte that you shall give such other preferrements as their former paines have de-

served, and in all matters of importance we require you to call them to consultacion and to proceede therein with their advice; and wee doe give further power and authority to you, to give the oathe of Counsellor to such as are now named, or any other oathe in the like case, accordinge to your direccion. Provided that they shall not have, single nor together, anie bindinge or negative voice or power uppon your conclusions but doe give you full authority, uppon just occasion to sequester any of them from the execucion of any place whatsover, and to depute another thereunto untill significacion unto us be here made:

5. You shall have power and authority to dispose and graunte any other officer or commaunds whatsoever, either of governement or warr, except such as are already disposed of by us to any persons of rancke or merite (adventurers beings first regarded), accordinge to your discrecion and so discharge or revoke the same or to sequester any so made or constituted by us.

6. You shall take principall order and care for the true and reverent worship of God that his worde be duely preached and his holy sacraments administred accordinge to the constitucions of the Church of England in all fundamentall pointes, and his ministers had in due observance and respecte agreeable to the dignity of their callinge. And that all atheisme, prophanes, popery, or schisme be exemplarily punished to the honor of God and to the peace and safety of his Church, over which, in this tendernes and infancy, you must be especially solicitous & watchefull.

7. You shall, with all propensenes and diligence, endeavour the conversion of the natives to the knowledge and worship of the true God and their redeemer Christ Jesus, as the most pious and noble end of this plantacion, which the better to effect you must procure from them some convenient nomber of their children to be brought up in your language and manners, and if you finde it convenient, we thinke it reasonable you first remove from them their Iniocasockes or Priestes by a surprise of them all and

detaininge them prisoners, for they are so wrapped up in the fogge and miserie of their iniquity and so tirrified with their continuall tirrany, chained under the bond of deathe unto the divell that while they live amounge them to poison and infecte them their mindes, you shall never make any great progres into this glorious worke, nor have any civill peace or concurre with them. And in case of necessity or conveniency, we pronounce it not crueltie nor breache of charity to deale more sharpely with them and to proceede even to dache [death?] with these murtherers of soules and sacrificers of God's images to the divill, referringe the consideracion of this as a waighty matter of important consequence to the circumstances of the busines and place in your discrecion.

8. You shall for capitall and criminal justice in case of rebellion and mutiny and in all such cases of [provident (?)] necessity, proceede by martiall lawe accordinge to your comission as of most dispatch and terror and fittest for this governement; and in all other causes of that nature as also in all matters of civill justice, you shall finde it properest and usefullest for your governement to proceede rather as a chauncelor than as a judge, rather uppon the naturall right and equity then uppon the nicenes and lettre of the lawe which perplexeth in this tender body, rather then dispatcheth all causes so that a summary and arbitrary way of justice discreetely mingled with those gravities and fourmes of magistracy as shall in your discrecion seeme aptest for you and that place, wilbe of most use both for expedicion and for example:

9. You shall for the more regard and respect of your place, to begett reverence to your authority and to refresh their mindes that obey the gravity of those lawes under which they were borne; at your discrecion use such fourmes and ensignes of governement as by our lettres pattents wee are enabled to grant unto you; as also the attendance of a guarde uppon your person, and in all such like cases you shall have power to make, adde or

distinguishe any lawes or ordinances at your discrecion accordinge to the authority limited in your comission.

10. You shall, for the choice of plantacions observe two generall rulles: that you rather seeke to the sun then from it, which is under God the first cause both of health and riches; and that such places which you resolve to build and inhabite uppon have at the leaste one good outlett into the sea & fresh water to the land; that it be a dry and wholesome earth and as free from woode as possiblie you may, whereby you may have roome to discover about you and unshady ground to plant nere you.

11. You must in every plantacion principally provide of your owne a common graunge and storehowse of corne, besides that which you will obtaine by tribute or trade with the natives.

12. In the distribucion of your men accordinge to these advises and relacions which wee have receaved, we advise you to continue the plantacion at James Towne with a convenient nomber of men, but not as your situacion or citty, because the place is unwholsome and but in the marish of Virginia, and to keepe it onely as a fitt porte for your shippes to ride before to arive and unlade att; butt neither shall you make it your principall storehowse or magazin either of armes, victualls or goods, but because it is so accessable with shippinge that an enemy may be easily uppon you with all the provision of ordinance and municion and it is not to be expected that anie fortificacion there can endure an enemy that hath the leasure to sitt downe before it.

13. The place you chose for your principall residence and seate to have your catle, provisions of corne, foode, and magazin of other municion in, as your greatest strength, trust and retraite, must be removed some good distance from any navigable river, except with small boates, by which no enemy shall dare to seeke your habitacion; and if in this place some good fortificacion be made to which no ordinance can be brought by water, if you be provided of victuall, you may dispute possession till a straunger be wearied and starved.

14. Above the over falles of the Kinges River it is likely you shall finde some convenient place to this purpose whither no enemy with ease can approache nor with ordinance at all but by land, with at howe greate disadvauntage he shall seeke when he must discover and fight at once uppon straightes, in woodes, at foordes, and places of all inconveniency, is easy to be considered; besides, you shall have the commodity of the braunche of the river to bringe downe your provisions from within the land in canooes and smalle boates in the River of Chechehounnack, neere unto you and not farre of another navagable outlett into the sea by the River of Pamaouke.

15. Foure dayes journey from your forte southewards is a towne called Ohonahorn seated where the River of Choanocki devideth it self into three braunches and falleth into the sea of Rawnocke in thirtie five degrees; this place, if you seeke by Indian guides from James forte to Winocke by water, from thence to Manqueocke, some twenty miles from thence to Caththega, as much and from thence to Oconahoen, you shall finde a brave and fruiteful seate every way unaccessable by a straunger enemy, much more abundant in pochon and in the grasse silke called Cour del Cherva and in vines, then any parte of this land knowne unto us. Here we suppose, if you make your principall and cheife seate, you shall doe most safely and richely because you are in the part of the land inclined to the southe, and two of the best rivers will supply you; besides you are neere to riche copper mines of Ritanoc and may passe them by one braunche of this river, and by another, Peccarecamicke, where you shall finde foure of the Englishe alive, left by Sir Walter Rawely, which escaped from the slaughter of Powhaton of Roanocke, uppon the first arrivall of our Colonie, and live under the proteccion of a wiroane called Gepanocon, enemy to Powhaton by whose consent you shall never recover them; one of these were worth much labour, and if you finde them not, yet seach [search?] into this countrey, it is more probable then towards the north.

16. These three habitacions seeme enoughe for the nomber of the people nowe transported, over every one of which you must appointe a discreete commaunder that shall sett your men to severall workes accordinge to their undertakings in the bookes by which they were receaved; in every one of these there must be builte a church and a storehowse and a parte of land sett out for corne for the publique and some allotted to the care of manuringe and preparinge thereof. In buildinge your towns you shall as easily keepe decorous and order as confusion; and so you shall prepare for ornament and safety at once, for every streete may answere one another and all of them the markett place or storehowse in the midle which at the leaste must be paved and made firme and dry.

17. Your enemies can be but of two sortes, straungers and natives; for the first, your defence must be uppon advauntage of the place and way unto it, for fortes have no other use but that a fewe men may defend and dispute their footinge with them against a greater nomber and to winne time which, if you can do, a stranger cannot longe abide where he must bringe all his releis [relief?] with him, and he shall have no way to beseidge you but by blockinge you in and plantinge between you and the sea, to which if you have two outeletts he must be very able and powerfull that can do it; to prevent this you shall build some small forte that may discry the sea neere Cape Comforte, and there hold a reasonable garrison and keepe alwaies watch and longe boate that may be ready to take the alarum and able to cary away our men, and munition if you shall not be able to defend it. Besides it is not safe to lett any of the savages dwell betwene you and the sea least they be made guides to your enemies. To this commaunde wee desire Captaine Smith may be allotted aswell for his earnest desire as the greate confidence & trust that we have in his care & diligence.

18. The second enemy is the natives who can no way hurte you but by fire or by destroyinge your catle, or hinderinge your

workes by stealth or your passages in small nombers; and in this sorte of warr there is most perill if you be not very carefull, for if they may destroy but one harvest or burne your townes in the night they will leave you naked and exposed to famine and cold, and convey themselves into wodes where revenge wilbe as difficult as unnecessary; to prevent that you must keepe good watches in the fielde and suffer none of them to come nere your corne in those daungerous seasons; and continuall centinells without the walles or uttermost defences in the night; and you must give order that your catle be kept in heards waited and attended on by some small watch or so enclosed by them selves that they destroy not your corne and other seed provisions.

19. For Powhaton and his Weroances it is clere even to reason beside our experience that he loved not our neighbourhood and therefore you may no way trust him, but if you finde it not best to make him your prisoner yet you must make him your tributary, and all other his weroances about him first to acknowledge no other lord but Kinge James, and so we shall free them all from the tirrany of Powhaton . . . uppon them. Every lord of a province shall pay you and send you into your forte where you make your cheif residence so many measures of corne at every harvest, soe many basketts of dye, so many dozens of skins, so many of his people to worke weekely, and of every thinge somewhat, accordinge to his proporcion in greatenes of territory and men; by which meanes you shall quietly drawe to your selves an annuall revenue of every commodity growinge in that countrey and this tribute payd to you, for which you shall deliver them from the exeacions of Powhaton which are now burdensome, and protect and defend them from all their enemies; shall also be a meanes of clearinge much ground of wood and of reducing them to laboure and trade seinge for this rent onely they shall enjoye their howses, and the rest of their travell quietly and many other commodities and blessings of which they are yet insensible.

20. If you hope to winne them and to provide for your selves by

trade you wilbe deceaved, for already your copper is embased by your abundance and neglect of prisinge it and they will never feede you but for feare. Wherefore, if you perceave that they, uppon your landinge, fly up into the countrey and forsake their habitacion, you must seise into your custody half there corne and harvest and their Weroances and all other their knowne successors at once whom, if you intreate well and educate those which are younge and to succeede in the governement in your manners and religion, their people will easily obey you and become in time civill and Christian.

21. If you make freindship with any of these nations, as you must doe, choose to doe it with those that are farthest from you and enemies unto those amonge whom you dwell, for you shall have least occasion to have differences with them and by that meanes a suerer league of amity, and you shalbe suer of their trade partely for covetousnes and to serve their owne ends, where the copper is yett in his primary estimacion which Pohaton hath hitherto engrossed and partely for feare of constrainte. Monocon, to the east and head of our river, Powhatons enemy; and the Manahockes, to the northeast to the head of the River of Moyompo in the necke of the land to the west betweene our bay and the sea; Cathcatapeius, a greater Weroance then he is, also his enemy to the Southeast and South—he hath no freinde to the north; the Masawoymekes make continuall incursions uppon him and uppon all those that inhabite the Rivers of Bolus and Myomps and to the northwest; Pocoughtuwonough infecteth him with a terrible warr. With those you may hold trade and freindeship good cheape for their emotenes [remoteness?] will prevent all offence which must needes happen betweene us and them which we are mingled with to the North. At the head bay is a large towne where is store of copper and furres called Cataaneon that trade and discovery wilbe to greate purpose, if it may be setled yearely.

22. Such trade as you shall finde necessary or profitable for you

with the Indians you shall endeavour to drawe them to seeke of you and to bringe their commodities into your forte, which will greatly ease the imployment of many men, and this you may bringe to passe by seeminge to make litle estimacion of trade with them and by pretendinge to be so able to consist within your selves as that you neede care for nothinge of theires, but rather that you doe them a curtesy to spare such necessaries as they want as leetle iron tooles, or copper, or the like such as are convenient for traffique; and so one officer or two in every forte, whom you must onely appointe to be truncmasters, may dispatch the whole busines of trade which els will cost you many mens laboures if you seeke it far from home. And besides these you must, by proclamacion or edicte publiquely affixed, prohibite and forbidd uppon paine or punishement of your discrecion all other persons to trade or exchange for anythinge but such as shalbe necessarie for foode or clothinge; and uppon all such commodities of yours as shall passe away from you whatsoever, you must sett prises and values under which the trunckemaster must not trade, and so you shalbe such to uphold the reputacion of your commodity and to make your traffique rich, desired and certaine; over this truncemaster there must be appointed a cape merchant or officer belonginge to the store or provision house that must deliver by booke all such things as shalbe allowed for trade and receave and take an accounte of whatsover is retourned, accordinge to the prises therein sett, and so beinge booked must store them up, to the publique use of the colony.

23. You must constitute and declare some sharpe lawe with a penaltie thereon to restraine the trade of any prohibited goods, especially of swordes, pikeheads, gunnes, daggers, or any thinge of iron that may be turned against you, and in case of such offence punishe severely; have also especially regard that no arte or trade tendinge to armes in any wise, as smithey, carpentry,

of or such like, be taught the savages or used in their presence, as they may learne therein.

24. Havinge deduced your colony into severall seates and plantacions that may commodiously answere and receive one another, you must devide your people into tennes, twenties, & so upwards, to every necessary worke a competent nomber, over every one of which you must appointe some man of care and [skill] in that worke to oversee them and to take daily accounte of their laboures; and you must ordaine that every overseer of such a nomber of workemen deliver once a weeke an accounte of the wholle committed to his charge [to] the cheife governor or captaine of the fourte; and that they also once a moneth make the like accounte to you or your officer and that such goodes or provisions as are advanced or gotten above expence may be receaved and entred into the capemarchantes booke and so stored and preserved to the publique use of the colony. And thus you shall both knowe howe your men are imployed, what they gett & where it is, as also the measure of your provision and wealth.

25. For such of your men as shall attend any worke in or nere aboute every towne, you shall doe best to lett them eate together at seasonable howers in some publique place, beinge messed by sixe or five to a messe, in which you must see there bee equality and sufficient that so they may come and retourne to their worke without any delay and have no cause to complaine of measure or to excuse their idlenes uppon the dressinge or want of diett. You may well allowe them three howers in a somers day and two in the winter, and shall call them together by ringinge of a bell and by the same worne them againe to worke; for such as attend any labouer so farre from the forte, as they cannot returne at seasonable times, there must be a steward appointed that shall oversee there diett and provision, els thoughe you give every one a reasonalbe allowance for many dayes some will eate two meales at one & soe:

26. You shall give especiall order to the cheif commaunder of

every forte that the armes, powder and munition be well stored and looked into and that the men be disposed into severall companies for warr and captaines appointed over every fifty to traine them at convenient times and to teache them the use of their armes and weapons and they may knowe whether uppon all occasions and sudden attempts they shall repaire to find them in a readines.

27. You must take especiall care what relacions come into England and what lettres are written and that all thinges of that nature may be boxed up and sealed and sent to first to the Councell here, accordinge to a former instruccion unto the late president in that behalf directed; and that at the arivall and retourne of every shippinge you endeavour to knowe all the particuler passages and informacions given on both sides and to advertise us accordingly.

28. Whensoever you consult of any busines of importance, wee advise you to consider and deliberate all thinges patiently & willingly and to heare every man his oppinion and objeccion, but the resultants out of them or your owne determinacion what you intend to doe not to imparte to any whatsoever, but to such onely as shall execute it, and to them also under the sealle of your commaundement and but at the instant of their partinge from you or the execucion of your will.

29. Next after buildinge, husbandry and manuringe the countrey for the provision of life and conveniency, wee comend unto your care foure principall waies of enrichinge the colonies and providinge returne of commodity, of which you must be very solicitouse that our fleetes come not home empty nor laden with useles marchandize. The first is discovery either of the southe seas or royall mines, in the search of both which we must referre you to the circumstances of your peace and your owne discrecion; the second is trade whereby you recover all the commodities of those countreys that ly far of and yet are accessable by water; the third is tribute, by which you shall advaunce parte of what

soever the next lande can provide you can produce; the fourth is labour of your owne men in makinge wines, pitche, tarre, sope, ashes, steele, iron, pipestaves, in sowinge of hempe and flaxe, in gatheringe silke of the grasse, and providinge the worme and in fishinge for pearle, codd, sturgion, and such like.

30. Wee require you to call before you Captaine John Radcliffe and one . . . Webbe who hath complained by peticion delivered unto you of divers injuries and insolences done unto him in the governement of the said Captaine Radcliffe, and accordingly to heare the cause and doe justice in it as you shall finde reason in it your owne discrecion.

31. Whereas suite hath bine made unto us as for the retourne of Richard Potts, David Wiffin and Post Ginnet, and sufficient reasons declared to move us to graunte the same which hath bine agreed unto by the Councell assembled, wee require you to give them their licence to come backe by the next shippinge with such condicions or limitacions of retorne or otherwise as you shall thinke good.

32. Whereas peticion hath bine made by the friends of John Tavernor, capemarchant of the forte and store in Virginia, for his retorne uppon some urgent occasion and for some time into England, we require you to licence him so to do if it be his desire when you arive there; and we doe nominate and appointe Thomas Wittingham into his roome and office, beinge one in whose sufficiency and honesty we have greate confidence.

33. There beinge one George Liste, servant to John Woodall and sent over by him with a chest of cheurgery sufficiently furnished, we require you to give your licence to William Wilson, his fellowe, if the said George Liste doe stay with you, to come backe in this passage, the better to enfourme us what medicines and drugges are fittest to be provided for the use of the colonie against the next supply.

34. You shall be very wary of grantinge freedomes and of givinge your sealle to any but uppon good consideracion and greate

merite, least you make cheape the best way of our recompence; and in those you doe you shall give with such limitacions of retorne in reasonable time as in your discrecion shall seeme good.

35. If it shall please God that you should dy either in your way or in your governement (which his mercy forbid) before other order be taken by us therein, wee requier and commaund that the Councell there established open a blacke boxe, marked with the figure of one and sealed with our sealle, wherein they shall finde our determinacion concerninge the successor to the governement; and do, in His Majesties name, charge and commaund every person within the precincte of the Colony to give and yeild due obedience to him so named and appointed accordinge unto his commission unto him, directed as they will aunswere to the contrary at their uttermost perill.

36. Wee also requier you, the present Governor & all your successors, to keepe secret to your selves, unsealed and unbroken up, all such lettres, schedules and instruments and whatsoever wee shall deliver you soe under our sealle, especially two blacke boxes with divers markes wherein are our commissions in cases of death or other vacacion of the Governor untill such time as you shall find your self unlikely to live or determined to returne, uppon which occasions wee requier you that they be delivered before all the Councell to be opened successively after such death or departure out of Virginia of any Governor.

Provided that in all thinges herein contained, except onely the succession, wee doe by these our lettres instruccions binde you to nothinge so strictely but that uppon due consideracion and good reason, and uppon divers circumstances of time and place wherein we cannot here conclude, you may in your discrecion departe and dissent from them and change, alter or establishe, execute and doe all ordinances or acts whatsoever that may best conducte to the glory of God, the honor of our Kinge and nation to the good and perfect establishement of our Colony

Geven under our hands and Councell sealle the day of May, in the seaventh yeare of His Majesties ragne of England, Fraunce & Ireland and Scotland the two and fortithe.

Kingsbury, *Records of the Virginia Company of London*, Vol. III, pp. 12-24.

VIRGINIA COUNCIL. "INSTRUCTIONS, ORDERS AND CONSTITUCIONS . . . TO . . . SIR THOMAS WEST, KNIGHT, LORD LA WARR."

1609/10(?)

Instructions, orders and constitucions by way of advise sett downe, declared, propounded and delivered to the Right Honourable Sir Thomas West, Knight, Lord La Warr, Lord Governor and Capten Generall of Virginea and of the Colonies there planted and to be planted and of all other the inhabitants thereof, by us, His Majesties Counsell for the Companie of Adventurers and Planters in Virginea resident in England under the hands of some of us for the direccion of the affares of that countrey for his better disposinge and proceedinge in the government thereof, according to the authoritie and power given unto us by His Majesties lettres patents in that behalf, together with a copie of certaine of the cheifest instruccions which have bene formerlie given to Sir Thomas Gates, Knight, for his direccion, which coppie we have given to his Lordship to peruse and looke into but leave it to his discretion to use and put them in execution or to beare to be advised or directed by them further then in his owne discretion he shall thinke meete.

We, the said Councell, havinge considered the great & zealous affeccion which you, Sir Thomas West, Knight, Lord Lawarr, have many wayes manifested unto us and for the furtherance and advaunceinge of the plantacion of Virginea have therefore by our commission under the handes of some of us, constituted you to be Lord Governor and Captaine Generall of Virginea and for your more safe and deliberate proceedinge in your goverment there, have advised, constituted & agreed uppon divers instructions followinge, vizt:

1. First, we require your Lordship to take into your charge our fleete consistinge of three good shippes with the masters, mariners, sailors and one hundred and fiftie landmen goinge in them

to be transported under your commaund with what speed conveniently you maye unto Virginea and with the first winde to sett saile for that place and in your passage thither not to lande or touche uppon anye of the Kinge of Spaine his dominions by him quietly possessed without the licence of the governour of such place first obtained, unles by necessitie of winde and weather you shalbe forced thereunto; in which passage you shall holde councell with the masters, pilates and men of best experience what way is safest and fitt for you to take for your arrivinge in Virginea.

2. Your Lordships beinge landed there, we wishe you should (with what convenientcy you may by proclamacion made) call into some publique place all the governors, officers and other His Majesties subjects, aswell already seated there as transported with you, to whom you shall manifest your commission and cause it to be publiquely read to them, to the end His Majesties pleasure may be knowne as alsoe our choise in establishinge your Lordship Governor of Virginea and of the plantacion there; and that the President, Counsell and Colony there may take notice of our revocacion of all former kindes and formes of goverment, constituted or confirmed, and that they accordingely may yeild due obedience unto you, theire Lord Governor and Captaine Generall, at which time we holde it fitt you tender unto every of them the oath of supremacy to be by them taken whereby they shall manifest theire obedience and loyaltie to His Majestie and you thereby the better assured of theire fidelities as alsoe to be the rather encouraged to comitt matter of counsell and charge unto them; att which time alsoe your Lordship shall, in our opinions, doe well to give generall commaundement that all former private or publique quarels, greivancs or grudgs be from thenceforth from amongest them utterly abbandoned and forgotten and they willingly embrace peace and love as becommeth Christians without discention or hindrance to the common good or quiet.

3. Moreover, your Lordship shall demaunde and resume into your hands all former commissions and all instructions and publique instruments given or sent unto them and all bookes and records whatsoever of all the proceedings untill this time and dispose of all theire offices and places in the future accordinge to your discretion; except the office of Leiuetennante Governor, which your Lordship is by your commission to bestowe upon Sir Thomas Gates, if he shalbe there to execute the same, and office of Marshall uppon Sir Thomas Dale, at this cominge thither, and the office of Admirall upon Sir George Sumers, if he shalbe there, and the office of Viceadmirall upon Capten Newport, he beinge there to supplye the said place.

4. Your shippes beinge discharged of theire provision, we wishe that they, the seamen and soe manie others as shalbe needfull for that worke, be, with what convenient speed you may, employed to theire fishinge for sturgeons and other fish; which done we desier your Lordship should make up the residue of theire fraight with divers of the best severall patternes of the land, commodities that you can gett there havinge regarde more to the goodnes and qualitie of them then to the quantity; and to retorne the said shippes for England with as quick dispatch as you may for easinge of the Companie of Adventurers of the charge both of wages of the said shippes, seamen and victualls which they must be att untill they retorne.

5. After your Lordship is settled in your governement, we thinke it very behofefull that you employ soe many of your people as shalbe needfull in sowing, setting and plantinge of corne and such rootes for foode as you for your better provision, sustentacion and maintennance shall thinke meete to be planted.

6. As touchinge your landmen, we thinke fitt your Lordship should reduce them all into severall bandes and companies of fifties or more when you thinke good and to committ the charge of them to severall officers and captaines to be exercised and trained up in martiall manner and warlike discipline.

7. Your Lordship is to take principall order and care for the true worship and service of God as by havinge the Gospell preched, frequent prayers and the sacraments often administred as becommeth Christians. And that such your ministers and preachers as shalbe with you be had in due respect agreable to theire dignitie and callinge and that your Lordship, with the counsell of your said prechers and ministers, doe, as occasion shall be offered, proceede in punishinge of all atheisme, prophanisme, popery and scisme by exemplary punishment to the honor of God and to the peace and safety of his church over which in this tendernes and infancy your Lordship must be especially solicitous and watchfull.
8. It is very expedient that your Lordship with all diligence indeavor the conversion of the natives and savages to the knowledge and worship of the true God and theire redemer Christ Jesus as the most pious and noble end of this plantacion; which the better to effecte you are to procure from them some of theire children to be brought up in our language and manners and, if you finde it convenient, we thinke it necesserie you first remove from them the iniocхарактерcocks or priests by a surprise of them and detaninge them prisoners and in case they shalbe willfull and obstinate then to send over some three or foure of them into England, we may endevor theire conversion here.
9. We holde it requisite that your Lordship in causes of civill justice, proceede rather as a counsellor then as a judge; that is to saie, rather uppon the right and equitie of the thinge in demaunde then uppon the nicenes and letter of the lawe, which perplexeth in this tender body rather then dispatcheth causes. Soe that a summary and arbitrary way of justice, mingled with discreet formes of magistracy as shall in your discretion seeme aptest for your Lordship to exercise in that place, wilbe of most use both for expedicion and example and for criminall causes, you are to deale therein according to your comission and good discretion;

10. That your Lordship doe not permitt any shippe or vessell to trade or traffique within your precincte to carrie from thence any commodities or marchandizes without warrant brought you or sent to your Lordship from the Councell for the Company of Adventurers under the Councell seale.

11. We doe require your Lordship that with what possible speed and conveniency you may, after you are setled, you appointe a convenient number with guides and some discreete commaunder to discover northwest, south and southwest, beyonde the faulls ten or twelve dayes journey, and that assone as may be your Lordship send unto us the narracion of that voyage what rivers, lakes or seas they finde or here of with the circumstanc there unto belonginge.

12. If Sir Thomas Gates be there arived and Sir George Sommers and Capten Newport, or any of them, that your Lordship doe give unto Sir Thomas Gates the place or office of Leiuetennant Governor to your Lordship duringe the time of your Lordship and his abode there together, and in your Lordships absence he beinge there to be your deputy and cheif generall and commaunder of the whole Colonye and Companie, and to rule and governe according to suche instructions as your Lordship shall limitt and appointe him; and that Sir George Sommers may have the office of Cheif Admirall under your Lordship and that Sir Ferdinando Weyneman may have the office of Master of the ordinance, and that Capten Newport may have the office of Viceadmirall unto your Lordship.

13. Your Lordship must take especiall care what relacions come into England and what lettres are written & that all things of that nature may be boxed up and sealed and sent first to the Counsell here, accordinge to a former instruction unto the late Governor in that behalf directed; and that att the arrival and retorne of every shippinge you endeavor to knowe all the particuler passages and informacions given on both sides and to advertise us accordingly.

14. Last of all, for temporall goverment & perticuler proceedinge in your plantacion, in respect of the shortnes of time, we commende unto your Lordship the copie of some of the cheifest of the old instruccions before mencioned to have bene formerly delivered to Sir Thomas Gates, to be used or refused as you shall in your wisdome thinke fitt, neither is or meanes to tie your Lordship to the stricte perfourmance of theis newe instructions but as occasion of time, place or necessetie shall requir your Lordship may doe therein as shall seeme best in your owne discretion. Southampton, Pembroke, Philip Mountgomery, Edward Cecill, Walter Cope, Dudly Diggs, William Rumney, Thomas Smith, Robert Drewrye, Robert Maunsell, Baptist Hicks, Christofer Brooke.

The copie of the old instruccions which were formerly with others delivered to Sir Thomas Gates, Knight, att his goinge to Virginea for his direccion in his govermcnt there, and noew are by us, His Majesties Councill for the Companie of Adventurers for Virginea, given to the Right Honourable, the Lord La Warr to looke into and advise on and at his discretion to use [or] forbeare to put them in execucion.

Such of the old instructions which were formerly given to Sir Thomas Gates, Knight, and nowe delivered to the Lord La Warre, beginne att the ninth instruccion in the articles in thi booke which by waye of advise were sett down to the said Sir Thomas Gates and soe are written ontill you come to the thirtith instruccion which 30th, 31, 32 & 33 instructions are not given his Lordship but the 34th is given him, but not the 35 nor 36, but the effect of the provisoe followinge is given.

Kingsbury, Vol. III, pp. 24-29.

THE THIRD CHARTER

March 12, 1612

James, by the grace of God [King of England, Scotland, France and Ireland, Defender of the Faith;] to all to whom [these presents shall come,] greeting. Whereas at the humble suite of divers and sundry our lovinge subjects, aswell adventurers as planters of the First Colonie in Virginia, and for the propagacion of Christian religion and reclayminge of people barbarous to civilitie and humanitie, we have by our lettres patent bearing date at Westminster the three and twentieth daie of May in the seaventh yeare of our raigne of England, Frannce and Ireland, and the twoe and fortieth of Scotland, given and grannted unto them, that they and all suche and soe manie of our loving subjects as shold from time to time for ever after be joyned with them as planters or adventurers in the said plantacion, and their successors for ever, shold be one body politique incorporated by the name of The Treasorer and Planters of the Cittie of London for the First Colonie in Virginia;

And whereas allsoe for the greater good and benefitt of the said Companie and for the better furnishing and establishing of the said plantacion we did further [give], grannte and confirme by our said lettres patent unto the said Treasorer and Companie and their successors for ever, all those landes, contries and territories scituate, lyeing and being in that part of America called Virginia, from the point of land called Cape [or] Pointe Comfort all along the seacoste to the northward twoe hundred miles, and from the said point of Cape Comfort all along the seacoste to the sowthward twoe hundred miles, and all the space and circuit of land lying from the sea coste of the precinct aforesaid up or into the land throughout from sea to sea, west and northwest, and allso all the islandes lying within one hundred miles along the coast of both the seas of the precinct aforsaid, with diverse other grannts, liberties, franchises, preheminences, privileges, proffitts, benefitts, and commodities, grannted in and by our said lettres patent to the said Tresorer and Companie, and their successors, for ever:

Now for asmuchas we are given to undestande that in these seas adjoyning to the said coast of Virginia and without the compasse of those twoe hundred miles by us soe grannted unto the said Treasurer and Companie as aforesaid, and yet not farr distant from the said Colony in Virginia, there are or may be divers islandes lying desolate and uninhabited, some of which are already made knowne and discovered by the industry, travell, and expences of the said Company, and others allsoe are supposed to be and remaine as yet unknowen and undiscovered, all and every of which itt maie importe the said Colony both in safety and pollecy of trade to populate and plant, in regard where of, aswell for the preventing of perill as for the better comodity and prosperity of the said Colony, they have bin humble suitors unto us that we wold be pleased to grannt unto them an inlardgement of our said former lettres patent, aswell for a more ample extent of their limitts and territories into the seas adjoyning to and uppon the coast of Virginia as allsoe for some other matters and articles concerning the better government of the said Company and Collony, in which point our said former lettres patents doe not extende soe farre as time and experience hath found to be needfull and convenient:

We, therefore, tendring the good and happy successe of the said plantacion both in respect of the generall weale of humane society as in respect of the good of our owne estate and kingedomes, and being willing to give furtherannt untoall good meanes that may advance the benefitt of the said Company and which maie secure the safety of our loving subjects, planted in our said Colony under the favour and proteccion of God Almighty and of our royall power and authority, have therefore of our especiall grace, certein knowledge and mere mocion, given, grannted and confirmed, and for us, our heires and successors we doe by theis presents, give, grannt and confirme unto the said Treasurer and Company of Adventurers and Planters of the said Citty of London for the First Colony in Virginia, and to their heires and successors for ever, all and singuler the said iselandes [whatsoever] scituat and being in anie part of the said ocean bordering upon the coast of our said First Colony in Virginia and being within three hundred leagues of anie the partes hertofore grannted to the said Treasorer and Company in our said former lettres patents as aforesaid, and being within or betweene the one and fortie and thirty degrees of Northerly latitude, together with all and singuler [soils] landes, groundes, havens, ports, rivers, waters, fishinges, mines and mineralls, aswell royal mines of gold and silver as other mines and mineralls, perles, precious stones, quarries, and all and singuler other commodities, jurisdiccions, royalties, priviledges, franchises and preheminences, both within the said tract of lande uppon the maine and allso within the said iselandes and seas adjoyning, whatsoever, and thereunto or there abouts both by sea and land being or scituat; and which, by our lettres patents, we maie or cann grannt and in as ample manner and sort as we or anie our noble progenitors have heretofore grannted to anie person or persons or to anie Companie, bodie politique or corporate or to any adventurer or adventurers, undertaker or undertakers of anie discoveries, plantacions or traffique, of, in, or into anie foreigne parts whatsoever, and in as lardge and ample manner as if the same were herein particularly named, mencioned and expressed: provided allwaies that the said iselandes or anie the premisses herein mencioned and by theis presents intended and meant to be grannted be not already actually possessed or inhabited by anie other Christian prince or estate, nor be within the bounds, limitts or territories of the Northerne Colonie, hertofore by us grannted to be planted by divers of our loving subjects in the northpartes of Virginia. To have and to hold, possesse and injoie all and singuler the said iselandes in the said ocean seas soe lying and bordering uppon the coast or coasts of the territories of the said First Colony in Virginia as aforesaid, with all and singuler the said soiles, landes and groundes and all and singular other the premisses heretofore by theis presents grannted, or mencioned to be grannted, to them, the said Treasurer and Companie of Adventurers and Planters of the Cittie of London for the First Colonie in Virginia, and to their heires, successors and assignes for ever, to the sole and proper use and behoofe of them, the said Treasurer and Companie and their heires, successores and assignes for ever; to be holden of us, our heires and successors as of our mannor of Eastgreenwich, in free and common soccage and not in capite, yealding and paying therefore, to us, our heires and successors, the fifte part of the oare of all gold and silver which shalbe there gotten, had or obteined for all manner of services, whatsoever.

And further our will and pleasure is, and we doe by theis presents grannt and confirme for the good and welfare of the said plantacion, and that posterity maie hereafter knowe whoe have adventured and not bin sparing of their purses in such a noble and generous accion for the generall good of theire cuntrie, and at the request and with the consent of the Companie aforesaid, that our trusty and welbeloved subjects.[19]

George, Lord Archbishopp of Canterbury
Gilbert, Earle of Shrewsberry
Mary, Countesse of Shreweshbeiry
Elizabeth, Countesse of Derby
Margarett, Countesse of Comberland
Henry, Earle of Huntingdon
Edward, Earle of Beddford
Lucy, Countesse of Bedford
Marie, Countesse of Pembroke

[19]Stith gives the following names only: "George, Lord Archbishop of Canterbury, Henry, Earl of Huntington, Edward, Earl of Bedford, Richard, Earl of Clanrickard, &c." The following names in brackets are taken from the text in Brown's *Genesis*.

Richard, Earle of Clanrickard
Lady Elizabeth Graie
William, Lord Viscount Cramborne
William, Lord Bishopp of Duresme
Henry, Lord Bishopp of Worceter
John, Lord Bishopp of Oxonford
William, Lord Pagett
Dudley, Lord North
Franncis, Lord Norries
William, Lord Knollis
John, Lord Harrington
Robert, Lord Spencer
Edward, Lord Denny
William, Lord Cavendishe
James, Lord Hay
Elianor, Lady Cave [Carre]
Maistres Elizabeth Scott, widdow
Edward Sackvill, Esquier
Sir Henry Nevill, of Aburgavenny, Knight
Sir Robert Riche, Knight
Sir John Harrington, Knight
Sir Raphe Wimwood, Knight
Sir John Graie, Knight
Sir Henry Riche, Knight
Sir Henry Wotton, Knight
Peregrine Berly, Esquier [Berty]
Sir Edward Phelipps, Knight, Maister of the Rolls
Sir Moile Finche, Knight
Sir Thomas Mansell, Knight
Sir John St. John, Knight
Sir Richard Spencer, Knight
Sir Franncis Barrington, Knight
Sir George Carie of Devonshire, Knight
Sir William Twisden, Knight
Sir John Leveson, Knight
Sir Thomas Walsingham, Knight
Sir Edward Care, Knight
Sir Arthure Manwaringe, Knight
Sir Thomas Jermyn, Knight
Sir Valentine Knightley, Knight
Sir John Dodderidge, Knight
Sir John Hungerford, Knight
Sir John Stradling, Knight
Sir John Bourchidd, Knight [Bourchier]
Sir John Bennett, Knight
Sir Samuel Leonard, Knight
Sir Franncis Goodwin, Knight
Sir Wareham St. Legier, Knight
Sir James Scudamore, Knight
Sir Thomas Mildmaie, Knight
Sir Percivall Harte, Knight
Sir Percivall Willoughby, Knight
Sir Franncis Leigh, Knight
Sir Henry Goodere, Knight
Sir John Cutt, Knight
Sir James Parrett, Knight
Sir William Craven, Knight
Sir John Sammes, Knight
Sir Carey Raleigh, Knight
Sir William Maynard, Knight
Sir Edmund Bowyer, Knight
Sir William Cornewallis, Knight
Sir Thomas Beomont, Knight
Sir Thomas Cunningsby, Knight

Sir Henry Beddingfeild, Knight
Sir David Murray, Knight
Sir William Poole, Knight
Sir William Throgmorton, Knight
Sir Thomas Grantham, Knight
Sir Thomas Stewkley, Knight
Sir Edward Heron, Knight
Sir Ralph Shelten, Knight
Sir Lewes Thesam, Knight
Sir Walter Aston, Knight
Sir Thomas Denton, Knight
Sir Ewstace Hart, Knight
Sir John Ogle, Knight
Sir Thomas Dale, Knight
Sir William Boulstrod, Knight
Sir William Fleetwood, Knight
Sir John Acland, Knight
Sir John Hanham, Knight
Sir Roberte Meller, Knight [Millor]
Sir Thomas Wilford, Knight
Sir William Lower, Knight
Sir Thomas Lerdes, Knight [Leedes]
Sir Franncis Barneham, Knight
Sir Walter Chate, Knight
Sir Thomas Tracy, Knight
Sir Marmaduke Darrell, Knight
Sir William Harrys, Knight
Sir Thomas Gerrand, Knight
Sir Peter Freetchvile, Knight
Sir Richard Trevor, Knight
Sir Amias Bamfeild
Sir William Smith of Essex, Knight
Sir Thomas Hewett, Knight
Sir Richard Smith, Knight
Sir John Heyward, Knight
Sir Christopher Harris, Knight
Sir John Pettus, Knight
Sir William Strode, Knight
Sir Thomas Harfleet, Knight
Sir Walter Vaughan, Knight
Sir William Herrick, Knight
Sir Samuell Saltonstall, Knight
Sir Richard Cooper, Knight
Sir Henry Fane, Knight
Sir Franncis Egiok, Knight
Sir Robert Edolph, Knight
Sir Arthure Harries, Knight
Sir George Huntley, Knight
Sir George Chute, Knight
Sir Robert Leigh, Knight
Sir Richard Lovelace, Knight
Sir William Lovelace, Knight
Sir Robert Yaxley, Knight
Sir Franncis Wortley, Knight
Sir Franncis Heiborne, Knight
Sir Guy Palme, Knight
Sir Richard Bingley, Knight
Sir Ambrose Turvill, Knight
Sir Nicholas Stoddard, Knight
Sir William Gree, Knight
Sir Walter Coverte, Knight
Sir Thomas Eversfeild, Knight
Sir Nicholas Parker, Knight
Sir Edward Culpeper, Knight
Sir William Ayliffe, Knight, and
Sir John Keile, Knight
Doctor George Mountaine, Dean of Westminster
Lawrence Bohan, Docktor in Phisick
Anthony Hinton, Doctor in Phisick
John Pawlett
Arthure Ingram
Anthony Irby

John Weld
John Walter
John Harris
Anthony Dyott
William Ravenscrofte
Thomas Warre
William Hackwill
Lawrence Hide
Nicholas Hide
Thomas Stevens
Franncis Tate
Thomas Coventry
John Hare
Robert Askwith
George Sanndys
Franncis Jones
Thomas Wentworth
Henry Cromewell
John Arundell
John Culpeper
John Hoskins
Walter Fitz Williams
Walter Kirkham
William Roscarrock
Richard Carmerdon
Edward Carne
Thomas Merry
Nicholas Lichfeild
John Middleton
John Smithe, and
Thomas Smith, the sonnes of Sir Thomas Smith
Peter Franke
George Gerrand
Gregory Sprynte
John Drake
Roger Puleston
Oliver Nicholas
Richard Nunnington [Monyngton]
John Vaughan
John Evelin
Lamorock Stradling
John Riddall
John Kettleby
Warren Townsend
Lionell Cranfeild
Edward Salter
William Litton
Humfrey May
George Thorpe
Henry Sandys, and
Edwin Sandys, the sonnes of Sir Edwin Sandys
Thomas Conway
Captaine Owen Gwinn
Captaine Giles Hawkridge
Edward Dyer
Richard Connock
Benjamin Brand
Richard Leigh, and
Thomas Pelham, Esquiers
Thomas Digges, and
John Digges, Esquiers, the sonnes of Sir Dudley Diggs, Knight
Franncis Bradley
Richard Buckminster [Buck]
Franncis Burley
John Procter
Alexannder Whitakers
Thomas Frake, thelder, and
Henry Freake, thelder, Ministers of God's word
The mayor and citizens of Chichester
The mayor and jurates of Dover
The bailiffs, burgesses and comonalty of Ipswich

The mayor and comunalty of Lyme Regis
The mayor and comonalty of Sandwich
The wardens, assistants and companie of the Trinity House
Thomas Martin
Franncis Smaleman
Augustine Steward
Richard Tomlins
Humfrey Jobson
John Legate
Robert Backley [Barkley]
John Crowe
Edward Backley [Barkley]
William Flett [Fleet]
Henry Wolstenholme
Edmund Alleyn
George Tucker
Franncis Glanville
Thomas Gouge
John Evelin
William Hall
John Smithe
George Samms
John Robinson
William Tucker
John Wolstenholme, and
Henry Wolstenholme, sonnes of John Wolstenholme, Esquier
William Hodges
Jonathan Mattall [Nuttall]
Phinees Pett
Captaine John Kinge
Captaine William Beck
Giles Alington
Franncis Heiton, and
Samuell Holliland, gentleman
Richard Chamberlaine
George Chamberlaine
Hewett Staper
Humfrey Handford
Raph Freeman
George Twinhoe [Swinhoe]
Richard Pigott
Elias Roberts
Roger Harris
Devereux Wogan
Edward Baber
William Greenewell
Thomas Stilles [Shilds]
Nicholas Hooker
Robert Garsett
Thomas Cordell
William Bright
John Reynold
Peter Bartley
John Willett
Humfry Smithe
Roger Dye
Nicholas Leate
Thomas Wale
Lewes Tate
Humfrey Merrett
Roberte Peake
Powell Isaackson
Sebastian Viccars
Jarvis Mundes
Richard Warner
Gresham Hogan Warner
Daniell Deruley
Andrew Troughton

William Barrett
Thomas Hodges
John Downes
Richard Harper
Thomas Foxall
William Haselden
James Harrison
William Burrell
John Hodsall
Richard Fishborne
John Miller
Edward Cooke
Richard Hall, marchaunt
Richard Hall, ankersmith
John Delbridge
Richard Francklin
Edmund Scott
John Britten
Robert Stratt
Edmund Pond
Edward James
Robert Bell
Richard Herne
William Ferrers
William Millett
Anthony Abdy
Roberte Gore
Benjamin Decrow
Henry Tunberley [Timberly]
Humfrey Basse
Abraham Speckart
Richard Moorer
William Compton
Richard Poulsoune [Pontsonne]
William Wolaston
John Desmont, clothier [Beomont]
Alexannder Childe
William Fald, fishmonger
Franncis Baldwin
John Jones, marchant
Thomas Plomer
Edward Plomer, marchants
John Stoickden
Robert Tindall
Peter Erundell
Ruben Bourne
Thomas Hampton, and
Franncis Carter, citizens of London,

whoe since our said last lettres patent are become adventurers and have joined themselves with the former adventurers and planters of the said Companie and societie, shall from henceforth be reputed, deemed and taken to be and shalbe brethren and free members of the Companie and shall and maie, respectively, and according to the proportion and value of their severall adventures, have, hold and enjoie all suche interest, right, title, priviledges, preheminences, liberties, franchises, immunities, profitts and commodities whatsoever, in as lardge, ample and beneficiall manner to all intents, construccions and purposes as anie other adventures nominated and expressed in anie our former lettres patent, or anie of them have or maie have by force and vertue of theis presents, or anie our former lettres patent whatsoever.

And we are further pleased and we doe by theis presents grannt and confirm that[20]

Phillipp, Earle of Montgomery
William, Lord Paget
Sir John Harrington, Knight
Sir William Cavendish, Knight
Sir John Sammes, Knight
Sir Samuell Sandys, Knight
Sir Thomas Freke, Knight
Sir William St. John, Knight
Sir Richard Grobham, Knight
Sir Thomas Dale, Knight
Sir Cavalliero Maycott, Knight
Richard Martin, Esquier
John Bingley, Esquier
Thomas Watson, Esquier, and
Arthure Ingram, Esquier,

whome the said Treasurer and Companie have, since the said [last] lettres patent, nominated and sett downe as worthy and discreete persons fitt to serve us as Counsellors, to be of our Counsell for the said plantacion, shalbe reputed, deemed and taken as persons of our said Councell for the said First Colonie in such manner and sort to all intents and purposes as those whoe have bin formerly ellected and nominated as our Counsellors for that Colonie and whose names have bin or are incerted and expressed in our said former lettres patent.

And we doe hereby ordaine and grannt by theis presents that the said Treasurer and Companie of Adventurers and Planters, aforesaid, shall and maie, once everie weeke or oftener at their pleasure, hold and keepe a court and assembly for the better ordening [ordering] and government of the said plantacion and such thinges as shall concerne the same; and that anie five persons of the said Counsell for the said First Collonie in Virginia, for the time being, of which Companie the Treasurer or his deputie allwaies to be one, and the nomber of fifteene others at the least of the generality of the said Companie assembled

[20]Stith gives the following names only: "Philip, Earl of Mongomery, William, Lord Paget, Sir John Starrington, Knt. &c."

together in such court or assembly in such manner as is and hath bin heretofore used and accustomed, shalbe said, taken, held and reputed to be and shalbe a full and sufficient court of the said Companie for the handling, ordring and dispatching of all such casuall and particuler occurrences and accidentall matters of lesse consequence and waight, as shall from time to time happen, touching and concerning the said plantacion.

And that, nevertheles, for the handling, ordring and disposing of matters and affaires of great waight and importance and such as shall or maie in anie sort concerne the weale publike and generall good of the said Companie and plantacion as namely, the manner of government from time to time to be used, the ordring and disposing of the said possessions and the setling and establishing of a trade there, or such like, there shalbe held and kept everie yeare uppon the last Wednesdaie save one of Hillary, Easter, Trinity and Michaelmas termes, for ever, one great, generall and solemne assembly, which fower severall assemblies shalbe stiled and called The Fower Great and Generall Courts of the Counsell and Companie of Adventurers for Virginia; in all and every of which said great and generall Courts soe assembled our will and pleasure is and we doe, for us, our heires and successors forever, give and grannt to the said Treasurer and Companie and their successors for ever by theis presents, that they, the said Treasurer and Companie or the greater nomber of them soe assembled, shall and maie have full power and authoritie from time to time and att all times hereafter to ellect and choose discreet persons to be of our [said] Counsell for the said First Colonie in Virginia and to nominate and appoint such officers as theie shall thinke fitt and requisit for the government, managing, ordring and dispatching of the affaires of the said Companie; and shall likewise have full power and authority to ordaine and make such lawes and ordinances for the good and wellfare of the said plantacion as to them from time to time shalbe thought requisite and meete: soe allwaies as the same be not contrary to the lawes and statutes of this our realme of England; and shall in like manner have power and authority to expulse, disfranchise and putt out of and from their said Companie and societie for ever all and everie such person and persons as having either promised or subscribed their names to become adventurers to the said plantacion of the said First Colonie in Virginia, or having bin nominated for adventurers in theis or anie our lettres patent or having bin otherwise admitted and nominated to be of the said Companie, have nevertheles either not putt in anie adventure [at] all for and towards the said plantacion or els have refused and neglected, or shall refuse and neglect, to bringe in his or their adventure by word or writing promised within sixe monthes after the same shalbe soe payable and due.

And wheras the failing and nonpaiment of such monies as have bin promised in adventure for the advanncement of the said plantacion hath bin often by experience found to be danngerous and prejudiciall to the same and much to have hindred the progresse and proceeding of the said plantacion; and for that itt seemeth to us a thing reasonable that such persons as by their handwriting have engaged themselves for the payment of their adventures, and afterwards neglecting their faith and promise, shold be compellable to make good and kepe the same; therefore our will and pleasure is that in anie suite or suites comenced or to be comenced in anie of our courts att Westminster, or elswhere, by the said Treasurer and Companie or otherwise against anie such persons, that our judges for the time being both in our Court of Channcerie and at the common lawe doe favour and further the said suits soe farre forth as law and equitie will in anie wise suffer and permitt.

And we doe, for us, our heires and successors, further give and grannt to the said Tresorer and Companie, and their successors for ever, that theie, the said Tresorer and Companie or the greater part of them for the time being, so in a full and generall court assembled as aforesaid shall and maie, from time to time and att all times hereafter, for ever, ellect, choose and permitt into their Company and society anie person or persons, as well straungers and aliens borne in anie part beyond the seas wheresoever, being in amity with us, as our naturall liedge subjects borne in anie our realmes and dominions; and that all such persons soe elected, chosen and admitted to be of the said Companie as aforesaid shall thereuppon be taken, reputed and held and shalbe free members of the said Companie and shall have, hold and enjoie all and singuler freedoms, liberties, franchises, priviledges, immunities, benefitts, profitts and commodities, whatsoever, to the said Companie in anie sort belonging or apperteining as fully, freely [and] amplie as anie other adventurer or adventurers now being, or which hereafter att anie time shalbe, of the said Companie, hath, have, shall, maie, might or ought to have or enjoy the same to all intents and purposes whatsoever.

And we doe further of our speciall grace, certaine knowledge and mere mocion, for us, our heires and successors, give and grantt to the said Tresorer and Companie and their successors, for ever by theis present, that itt shalbe lawfull and free for them and their assignes att all and everie time and times hereafter, out of anie our realmes and dominions whatsoever, to take, lead, carry and transport in and into the said voyage and for and towards the said plantacion of our said First Collonie in Virginia, all such and soe manie of our loving subjects or anie other straungers that will become our loving subjects and live under our allegiance as shall willingly accompanie them in the said voyage and plantacion; with shipping, armour, weapons, ordinannce, munition, powder, shott, victualls, and all manner of merchandizes and wares, and all manner of clothing, implement, furniture, beasts, cattell, horses, mares, and all other thinges necessarie for the said plantacion and for their use and defence, and for trade with the people there and in passing and retourning to and froe, without paying or yealding anie subsedie, custome or imposicion, either inward or outward, or anie other dutie to us, our heires or successors, for the same, for the space of seven yeares from the date of theis present.

And we doe further, for us, our heires and successors, give and grannt to the said Treasurer and Companie and their successors for ever, by theis present, that the said Treasurer of the said Companie, or his deputie for the time being or anie twoe others of our said Counsell for the said First Colonie in Virginia for the time being, shall and maie attall times hereafter and from time to time, have full power and authoritie to minister and give the oath and oathes of supremacie and allegiannce, or either of them, to all and every person and persons which shall, at anie time and times hereafter, goe or passe to the said Colonie in Virginia:

And further, that itt shalbe likewise lawfull for the said Tresorer, or his deputy for the time, or anie twoe others of our said Counsell for the said First Colonie in Virginia, for the time being, from time to time and att all times hereafter, to minister such a formall oathe as by their discrescion shalbe reasonably devised, aswell unto anie person or persons imployed or to be imployed in, for, or touching the said plantation for their honest, faithfull and just dischardge of their service in all such matters as shalbe committed unto them for the good and benefitt of the said Company, Colonie and plantacion; as alsoe unto such other person or persons as the said Treasurer or his deputie, with twoe others of the said Counsell, shall thinke meete for the examinacion or clearing of the truith in anie cause whatsoever concerninge the said plantacion or anie business from thence proceeding or there unto proceeding or thereunto belonging.

And, furthermore, whereas we have ben certefied that diverse lewde and ill disposed persons, both sailors, souldiors, artificers, husbandmen, laborers, and others, having received wages, apparrell or other entertainment from the said Company or having contracted and agreed with the said Companie to goe, to serve, or to be imployed in the said plantacion of the said First Colonie in Virginia, have afterwards either withdrawen, hid or concealed themselves, or have refused to goe thither after they have bin soe entertained and agreed withall; and that divers and sundry persons allso which have bin sent and imployed in the said plantacion of the said First Colonie in Virginia at and upon the chardge of the said Companie, and having there misbehaved themselves by mutinies, sedition, and other notorious misde meanors, or having bin employed or sent abroad by the governor of Virginia or his deputie with some ship or pinnace for provisions for the said Colonie, or for some discoverie or other buisines and affaires concerning the same, have from thence most trecherouslie either come back againe and retorned into our realme of England by stelth or without licence of our Governor of our said Colonie in Virginia for the time being, or have bin sent hither as misdoers and offenders; and that manie allsoe of those persons after their retourne from thence, having bin questioned by our said Counsell here for such their misbehaviors and offences, by their insolent and contemptuous carriage in the presence of our said Counsaile, have shewed little respect and reverence, either to the place or authoritie in which we have placed and appointed them; and others, for the colouring of their lewdnes and misdemeanors committed in Virginia, have endeavored them by most vile and slanndrous reports made and divulged, aswell of the cuntrie of Virginia as alsoe of the government and estate of the said plantacion and Colonie, as much as in them laie, to bring the said voyage and plantacion into disgrace and contempt; by meanes where of not only the adventures and planters alreadie ingaged in the said plantacion have bin exceedingly abused and hindred, and a greate nomber of other our loving and welldisposed subjects otherwise well affected and inclyning to joine and adventure insoe noble, Christian and worthie an action have bin discouraged from the same, but allsoe the utter overthrow and ruine of the said enterprise hath bin greatlie indanngered which cannott miscarrie without some dishonor to us and our kingdome;

Now, for asmuch as it appeareth unto us that theis insolences, misdemeanors and abuses, not to be tollerated in anie civill government, have for the most part growne and proceeded inregard of our Counsaile have not anie direct power and authoritie by anie expresse wordes in our former lettres patent to correct and chastise such offenders, we therefore, for the more speedy reformacion of soe greate and enormous abuses and misdemeanors heretofore practised and committed, and for the preventing of the like hereafter, doe by theis present for us, our heires and successors, give and grannt to the said Treasurer and Companie, and their successors for ever, that itt shall and maie be lawfull for our said Councell for the said First Colonie in Virginia or anie twoe of them, whereof the said Tresorer or his deputie for the time being to be allwaies one, by warrant under their handes to send for, or cause to be apprehended, all and every such person and persons who shalbe noted or accused or found, att anie time or times here after, to offend or misbehave themselves in anie the offences before mencioned and expressed; and uppon the examinacion of anie such offender or offendors and just proofe made by oath taken before the Counsaile of anie such notorious misdemeanors by them committed as aforesaid; and allsoe uppon anie insolent, contemptuous or unreverent carriage and misbehavior to or against our said Counsell shewed or used by anie such person or persons soe called, convented and apearing before them as aforesaid; that in all such cases theie, our said Counsell or anie twoe of them for the time being, shall and maie have full power and authoritie either here to binde them over with good suerties for their good behaviour and further therein to proceed to all intents and purposes, as itt is used in other like cases within our realme of England; or ells att their discrescion to remannd and send back the said offenders or anie of them unto the said Colonie in Virginia, there to be proceeded against and punished as the Governor, deputie and Counsell there for the time being shall thinke meete; or otherwise, according to such lawes and ordinannces as are or shalbe in use there for the well ordring and good governement of the said Colonie.

And, for the more effectuall advanncing of the said plantacion, we doe further, for us, our heires and successors, of our especiall grace and favour, by vertue of our prorogative royall and by the assent and consent of the Lordes and others of our Privie Counsalle, give and grannte unto the said Tresorer and Companie full power and authoritie, free leave, libertie and licence to sett forth, errect and publishe one or more lotterie or lotteries to have continuance and to [endure] and be held for the space of one whole yeare next after the opening of the same, and after the end and expiracion of the said terme the said lotterie or lotteries to continue and be further kept, during our will and pleasure onely and not otherwise. And yet, nevertheles, we are contented and pleased, for the good and wellfare of the said plantacion, that the said Tresorer and Companie shall, for the dispatch and finishing of the said lotterie or lotteries, have six months warninge after the said yeare ended before our will and pleasure shall, for and on that behalfe, be construed, deemed and adjudged to be in anie wise altered and determined.

And our further will and pleasure is that the said lottery or lottaries shall and maie be opened and held within our cittie of London or in anie other cittie or citties, or ellswheare within this our realme of England, with such prises, articles, condicions and limitacions as to them, the said Tresorer and Companie, in their discreascions shall seeme convenient.

And that itt shall and may be lawfull to and for the said Tresorer and Companie to ellect and choose receivors, auditors, surveyors, comissioners, or anie other officers whatsoever, att their will and pleasure for the better marshalling and guiding and governing of the said lottarie or lottaryes; and that itt shallbe likewise lawfull to and for the said Tresorer and anie twoe of the said Counsell to minister unto all and everie such persons soe ellected and chosen for officers as aforesaid one or more oathes for their good behaviour, just and true dealing in and about the lottarie or lottaries to the intent and purpose that none of our loving subjects, putting in their monies or otherwise adventuring in the said generall lotterie or lottaries, maie be in anie wise defrauded and deceived of their said monies or evill and indirectlie dealt withall in their said adventures.

And we further grannt in manner and forme aforesaid, that itt shall and maie be lawfull to and for the said Treasurer and Companie, under the seale of our Counsell for the plantacion, to publishe or to cause and procure to be published by proclamacion or otherwise, the said proclamacion to be made in their name by vertue of theise present, the said lottarie or lotteries in all citties, townes, boroughts, throughfaires and other places within our said realme of England; and we will and commande all mayors, justices of peace, sheriffs, bayliffs, constables and other our officers and loving subjects whatsoever, that in noe wise theie hinder or delaie the progresse and proceeding of the said lottarie or lottaries but be therein and, touching the premisses, aiding and assisting by all honest, good and lawfull meanes and endevours.

And further our will and pleasure is that in all questions and dobts that shall arise uppon anie difficultie of construccion or interpretacion of anie thing conteined in theis or anie other our former lettres patent the same shalbe taken and interpreted in most ample and beneficiall manner for the said Tresorer and Companie and their successors and everie member there of.

And lastly we doe by theis present retific and confirme unto the said Treasorer and Companie, and their successors for ever, all and all manner of priviledges, franchises, liberties, immunities, preheminences, profitts and commodities whatsoever grannted unto them in anie our [former] lettres patent and not in theis present revoked, altered, channged or abridged. Although expresse mencion [of the true yearly value or certainty of the premises, or any of them, or of any other gift or grant, by us or any of our progenitors or predecessors, to the aforesaid Tresurer and Company heretofore made, in these Presents is not made; or any statute, act, ordinance, provisions, proclamation, or restraint, to the contrary thereof heretofore made, ordained, or provided, or any other matter, cause, or thing, whatsoever, to the contrary, in any wise, notwithstanding.]

In witnes whereof [we have caused these our letters to be made patents.] Wittnes our selfe att Westminster, the twelveth daie of March [1612] [in the ninth year of our reign of England, France, and Ireland, and of Scotland the five and fortieth.]

Per breve de privato sigillo, etc.

P. R. O. Chancery Patent Rolls (c. 66), 1709; Stith, Appendix, pp. 23-32; Hening, Vol. I, pp. 98-110.

VIRGINIA COMPANY. INSTRUCTIONS TO GEORGE YEARDLEY

(Sometimes called "The Great Charter")[21]

NOVEMBER 18, 1618

The Treasurer and Companie of Adventurers and Planters of the City of London for the First Colony in Virginia to Captain George Yeardley, Elect Governor of Virginia, and to the Council of State there being or to be, greeting:

Our former cares and endeavours have been chiefly bent to the procuring and sending people to plant in Virginia so to prepare a way and to lay a foundation whereon a flourishing state might, in process of time by the blessing of Almighty God, be raised. Now our trust being that under the goverment of you, Captain Yeardly, with the advice and assistance of the said Council of State, such public provisions of corn and cattle will again be raised as may draw on those multitudes who, in great abundance from diverse parts of the realm, were preparing to remove thither, if by the late decay of the said public store their hopes had not been made frustrate and their minds thereby clene discouraged. We have thought good to bend our present cares and consultations, according to the authority granted unto us from His Majesty under his Great Seal, to the setling there of a laudable form of government by majestracy and just laws for the happy guiding and governing of the people there inhabiting, like as we have already done for the well ordering of our courts here and of our officers and accions for the behoof of that plantation. And because our intent is to ease all the inhabitants of Virginia forever of all taxes and public burthens, as much as may be, and to take away all occasion of oppression

[21]There is no authority in these Instructions for the Governor to establish a General Assembly. There is, however, evidence in the Instructions to Wyatt (p. 123) that a "Commission" was given to Yeardley which granted this authority.

and corruption, we have thought fit to begin (according to the laudable example of the most famous common wealthes both past and present) to alot and lay out a convenient portion of public lands for the maintenance and support as well of magistracy and officers as of other public charges both here and there from time to time arising. We, therefore, the said Treasurer and Company, upon a solemn treaty and resolution and with the advice, consent and assent of His Majesties Council here of Virginia, being assembled in a great and general Court of the Council and Company of Adventurers for Virginia, require you, the said Governor and Council of Estate, to put in execution with all convenient speed a former order of our courts (which had been commended also to Captain Argal at his making Deputy Governor) for the laying and seting out by bounds and metes of three thousand acres of land in the best and most convenient place of the territory of James town in Virginia and next adjoining to the said town to be the seat and land of the Governor of Virginia for the time being, and his successors, and to be called by the name of the Governors Land, which Governors Land shall be of the freed grounds by the common labor of the people sent thither at the Companies charges, and of the lands formerly conquered or purchased of the Paspeheies and of other grounds next adjoining. In like sort we require you to set and lay out by bounds and metes other three thousand acres of good land within the territory of James town which shall be convenient, and in such place or places as in your discretions you shall find meet; which latter three thousand acres shall be and so called the Companies Land. And we require you, Captain Yeardley, that immediately upon your arrival you take unto you the guard assigned to Captain Argal at his going Deputy Governor, or sithence by him assumed, to be of your guard [for the better defence][22] of your Government; and that as well the said

[22]Editorial insertion by Kingsbury.

guard as also fifty other persons, now sent and transported with you, you place as tennants on the said Governors Land and that all other persons heretofore transported at the common charge of the Company since the coming away of Sir Thomas Dale, Knight, late Deputy Governor, be placed as tennants on the said Companies Lands. And we will and ordain that all the said tennants on the Governors and Companies Lands shall occupy the same to the half part of the profits of the said lands, so as the one half to be and belong to the said tennants themselves and the other half respectively to the said Governor and to us, the said Treasurer and Company and our successors. And we further will and ordain that of the half profits arising out of the said Companies Lands and belonging to us, the said Treasurer and Company, the one moiety be imploied for the entertainment of the said Councel of Estate there residing and of other public officers of the general Colony and plantation (besides the Governor), according to the proportion as hereafter we shall express and in the mean time as you in your discretions shall think meet. And the other moiety be carefully gathered, kept and shipped for England for the public use of us, the said Treasurer and Company and our successors. And we will and ordain that, out of the half profits of the said Companies Lands to us belonging, one fifth part be deducted and alotted for the wages of the bailiffs and other officers which shall have the oversight and goverment of the said tenants and lands, and the dividing, gathering, keeping or shiping of the particular moiety of the profits belonging either to the said Council and officer there or to us, the said Treasurer and Company and our successors, as aforesaid. Provided alwaies, that out of the said Companies Land a sufficient part be exempted and reserved for the securing and wintering of all sorts of cattle which are or shall be the public stock and store of the said Company. And forasmuch as our intent is to establish one equal [blank of several lines][23] planta-

[23]Editorial note by Kingsbury.

tions, whereof we shall speak afterwards, be reduced into four cities or burroughs, namely: the cheif city called James town, Charles City, Henrico, and the Burrough of Kiccowtan. And that in all these foresaid cities or burroughs and ancient adventurers and planters which [were] transported thither, with intent to inhabit at their own costs and charges, before the coming away of Sir Thomas Dale, Knight, and have so continued during the space of three years, shall have upon a first division, to be afterward by us augmented, one hundred acres of land for their personal adventure and as much for every single share of twelve pound ten shillings paid [for such share], allotted and set out to be held by them, their heirs and assigns, forever. And that for all such planters as were brought thither at the Companies charge to inhabit there, before the coming away of the said Sir Thomas Dale, after the time of their service to the Company on the common Land agreed shall be expired, there be set out one hundred acres of land for each of their personal adventurers to be held by them, their heirs and assigns, for ever; paying for every fifty acres the yearly free rent of one shilling to the said Treasurer and Company and their successors, at one entire payment on the feast day of St Michael the Archangel, for ever. And in regard that by the singular industry and virtue of the said Sir Thomas Dale the former difficulties and dangers were in greatest part overcome to the great ease and security of such as have been since that time transported thither, we do, therefore, hereby ordain that all such persons as sithence the coming away of the said Sir Thomas Dale have at their own charges been transported thither to inhabit, and so continued as aforesaid, there be allotted and set out upon a first division fifty acres of land to them and their heirs, for ever, for their personal adventure, paying a free rent of one shilling yearly in manner aforesaid.

And that all persons which since the going away of the said Sir Thomas Dale have been transported thither at the Companies charges, or which hereafter shall be so transported, be placed as tenants on the Companies lands for term of seven years, occupy the same to the half part of the profits as is abovesaid. We therefore will and ordain that other three thousand acres of land be set out in the fields and territory of Charles City; and other three thousand acres of land in the fields and territories of Henrico; and other three thousand acres of land in the fields and territory of Kiccowtan, all which to be and be called the Companies Lands and to be occupied by the Companies tenants for half profits as afore said. And that the profits belonging to the Company be disposed by their several moieties in the same manner as before set down touching the Companies lands in the territory of James Town with like allowance to the bailies and reservation of ground for the common store of cattle in those several places, as is there set down. And our will is that such of the Companies tenants as already inhabite in those several cities or burroughs be not removed to any other city or burrough but placed on the Companies Lands belonging to those cities or burroughs where they now inhabite; provided alwaies, that if any private person, without fraud or injurious intent to the public at his own charges, have freed any of the said lands formerly appointed to the Governor, he may continue and inhabite there till a valuable recompence be made him for his said charges. And we do hereby ordain that the Governors house in James town, first built by Sir Thomas Gates, Knight, at the charges and by the servants of the Company, and since enlarged by others by the very same means, be and continue for ever the Governors house, any pretended undue grant made by misinformation and not in a general and quarter court to the contrary in anywise notwithstanding. And to the intent that godly, learned and painful ministers may be placed there for the service of Almighty God & for the spiritual benefit and comfort of the people, we further will and ordain that in every of those cities or burroughs the several quantity of one hundred acres of land be set out in quality of glebe land toward the maintenance of the several ministers of the parishes to be there limited; and for a further supply of their maintenance there be raised a yearly standing and certain contribution out of the profits growing or renuing within the several farmes of the said parish; and so as to make the living of every minister, two hundred pounds sterling per annum or more as hereafter there shall be cause. And for a further ease to the inhabitants of all taxes and contributions for the support and entertainment of the particular magistrates and officers and of other charges to the said citys and burroughs, respectively belonging, we likewise will and ordain that within the precincts or territories of the said cities and burroughs shall be set out and alotted the several quantities of fifteen hundred acres of land to be the common land of the said citie or burrough, for the uses aforesaid, and to be known and called by the name of the Cities or Burroughs Land. And whereas, by a special grant and licence from His Majesty, a general contribution over this realm hath been made for the building and planting of a college for the training up of the children of those infidels in true religion, moral virtue and civility, and for other godly uses, we do, therefore, according to a former grant and order, hereby ratifie, confirm and ordain that a convenient place be chosen and set out for the planting of a university at the said Henrico in time to come and that in the mean time preparation be there made for the building of the said college for the children of the infidels, according to such instructions as we shall deliver; and we will and ordain that ten thousand acres, partly of the lands they impaled and partly of other land within the territory of the said Henrico, be alotted and set out for the endowing of the said university and college with convenient possessions. Whereas also we have heretofore, by order of court in consideration of the long, good and faithful service done by you, Captain George Yeardley, in our said Colony and plantation of Virginia, and in reward there of as also in regard of two single shares in money paid into our treasury, granted unto you, the said Captain Yeardley, all that parcel of marsh ground called Weynock and also one other peice and percel of land adjoining to the same marsh called by the Natives *Konwan,* one parcel whereof abutteth upon a creek there called Mapscock towards the east, and the other parcel thereof towards a creek there called Queens Creek on the west and extendeth in breadth to landward from the head of the said creek called Mapscock up to the head of the said creek called Queens Creek (which creek called Queens Creek is opposite to that point there which is now called the Tobacco point and abutteth south upon the River and north to the Landward), all which several lands are or shall be henceforward accounted to be lying within the territory of the said Charles City and exceed not the quantity of two thousand and two hundred acres, we therefore, the said Treasurer and Company, do hereby again grant, ratifie and confirm unto you, the said Captain George Yeardley, the said several grounds and lands; to have and to hold the said grounds and lands to you, the said Captain George Yeardley, your heirs and assigns, for ever. And for the better encouragement of all sorts of necessary and laudable trades to be set up and exercised within the said four cities burroughs, we do hereby ordain that if any artizans or trademen shall be desirous rather to follow his particular art or trade then to be imploied in husbandry or other rural business, it shall be lawful for you, the said Governor and Councel, to alot and set out within any of the precincts aforesaid one dwelling house with four acres of land adjoining and held in fee simple to every said tradsman, his heirs and assigns for ever, upon condition that the said tradesman, his heirs and assigns do continue and exercise his trade in the said house paying only a free rent of four pence by the year to us, the said Treasurer and Company and our successors, at the feast of St Michael the Archangel, for ever. And touching all other particular plantations set out or like to be set out in convenient multitudes, either by divers of the ancient adventurers associating themselves together (as the Society of Smiths Hundred and Martins Hundred) or by some ancient adventurer or planter associating others unto him (as the plantation of Captain Samuel Argall and Captain John Martin and that by the late Lord La Warre advanced) or by some new adventurers joining themselves under one head (as the plantation of Christopher Lawne, Gentleman, and others now in providing), our intent being according to the rules of justice and good government to alot unto every one his due yet so as neither to breed disturbance to the right of others nor to interrupt the good form of government intended for the benefit of the people and strength of the Colony; we do therefore will and ordain that of the said particular plantations none be placed within five miles of the said former cities and boroughs, and that if any man, out of his own presumption or pleasure without special direction from us, hath heretofore done otherwise a convenient time be assigned him and then by your discretions to remove to some farther place by themselves, to be chosen with the allowance and assent of the Governor for the time being and the Council of Estate; and that the inhabitants of the said city or burrough too near unto which he or they were placed make him and them a valuable recompense for their charges and expence of time in freeing of grounds and building within those precincts; in like sort, we ordain that no latter particular plantation shall at any time hereafter be seated within ten miles of a former; we also will and ordain that no particular plantation be or shall be placed straglingly in divers places to the weakening of them, but be united together in one seat and territory that so also they may be incorporated by us into one body corporate and live under equal and like law and orders with the rest of the Colony; we will and ordain also for the preventing of all fraud in abusing of our grants, contrary to the intent and just meaning of them, that all such person or persons as have procured or hereafter shall procure grants from us in general words unto themselves and their associates or to like effect shall within one year after the date hereof deliver up to us in writing, under their hands and seals, as also unto you, the said Governor and Councel, what be or were the names of those their first associates; and if they be of the adventurers of us, the Company which have paid into our treasury money for their shares, that then they express in that their writing for how many shares they join in the said particular plantation, to the end a due proportion of land may be set out unto them and we the said Treasurer and Company be not defrauded of our due; and if they be not of the adventurers of the Company which have paid into our treasury money for their shares, yet are gone to inhabit there and so continue for three years, there be allotted and set out fifty acres of land for every such person paying a free rent of twelve pence the year, in manner aforesaid, and all such persons having been planted there since the coming away of Sir Thomas Dale; and forasmuch as we understand that certain persons, having procured such grants in general words to themselves and their associates or to like effect, have corruptly of late endeavoured for gain and worse respects to draw many of the ancient planters of the said four cities or burroughs to take grants also of them and thereby to become associated unto them with intent also by such means to overstrengthen their party; and thereupon have adventured on divers enormous courses tending to the great hurt and hindrance of the Colony; yea, and have also made grants of like association to masters of ships and mariners never intending there to inhabit, thereby to defraud His Majesty of the customs due unto him; we, to remedy and prevent such unlawful and greedy courses tending also directly to faction and sedition, do hereby ordain that it shall not be lawful for the grantees of such grants to associate to any other unto them then such as were their associates from the first time of the said grants, without express licence of us, the said Treasurer and Company, in a great general and quarter court under our seal obtained; and that all such after or under grants of association made or to be made by the said grantees shall be to all intents and purposes utterly void. And for as much as we understand that divers particular persons (not members of our Company), with their companies, have provided or are in providing to remove into Virginia with intent (as appeareth) by way of association to shroud themselves under the general grants last aforesaid, which may tend to the great disorder of our Colony and hinderance of the good government which we desire to establish, we do therefore hereby ordain that all such persons as of their own voluntary will and authority shall remove into Virginia, without any grant from us in a great general and quarter court in writing under our seal, shall be deemed (as they are) to be occupiers of our land, that is to say, of the common lands of us, the said Treasurer and Company; and shall yearly pay unto us for the said occupying of our land one full fourth part of the profits thereof till such time as the same shall be granted unto them by us in manner aforesaid, and touching all such as being members of our Company and adventurers by their monies paid into our treasury, shall either in their own person or by their agents, tennants or servants set up in Virginia any such particular plantation, tho with the privity of us, the said Treasurer and Company, yet without any grant in writing made in our said general quarter courts as is requisite, we will and ordain that the said adventurers or planters shall, within two year after the arrival of them or their company in Virginia, procure our grant in writing to be made, in our general quarter court and under our seal, of the lands by them possessed or occupied, or from thenceforth shall be deemed only occupiers of the common land, as is aforesaid, till such times as our said grant shall be obtained. We also not more intending the reformation of the errors of the said [24] than for advancing of them into good courses and therein to assist them by all good means, we further hereby ordain that to all such of the said particular

[24]Blank space.

[24] as shall truly fully observe the orders afore and hereafter specified there be alotted and set out, over and above our former grants, one hundred acres of glebe land for the Minister of every [24] and fifteen hundred acres of burough land for the public use of the said plantation; not intending yet hereby either to abridge or enlarge such grant of glebe or common land as shall be made in any of our grants in writing to any of the said particular plantations; we also will and ordain that the like proportion of maintenance out of the [24] and profits of the earth be made for the several ministers of the said particular plantations as have been before set down for the Ministers of the said former cities and burroughs; we will and ordain that the Governor for the time being and the said Council of Estate do justly perform or cause to be performed all such grants, covenants and articles as have or shall be in writing in our great and general quarter courts to any of the said particular plantations, declaring all other grants of lands in Virginia, not made in one of our great and general quarter courts, by force of His Majesties letters patents to be void. And to the end aforesaid we will and ordain that all our grants in writing under our seal, made in our great and general quarter courts, be entered into your records to be kept there in Virginia; yet directly forbiding that a charter of land granted to Captain Samuel Argal and his associates, bearing date the twentieth of March, 1616, be entered in your records or otherwise at all respected, forasmuch as the same was obtained by slight and cunning; and afterwards upon suffering him to go Governor of Virginia was by his own voluntary act left in our custody to be cancelled upon grant of a new charter which [24] We do also hereby declare that heretofore in one of our said general and quarter courts we have ordained and enacted and in this present court have ratified and confirmed these orders and laws following: that all grants of lands, privileges and liberties in Virginia hereafter to be made, be passed by indenture,

[24]Blank space.

a counterpart whereof to be sealed by the grantees and to be kept [25] the Companies [25] evidences; and that the Secretary of the Company have the engrossing of all such indentures; that no patents or indentures of grants of land in Virginia be made and sealed but in a full, general and quarter court, the same having been first thoroughly perused and approved under the hands of a select committee for that purpose [25] that all grants of [25] in Virginia to such adventurers as have heretofore brought in their money here to the treasury for their several shares, being of twelve pounds ten shillings the share, be of one hundred acres the share upon the first division and of as many more upon a second division, when the land of the first division shall be sufficiently peopled; and for every person which they shall transport thither within seven years after Midsummer Day, one thousand six hundred and eighteen, if he continue there three years or dye in the mean time after he is shiped it be of fifty acres the person upon the first division and fifty more upon a second division, the land of the first being sufficiently peopled, without paying any rent to the Company for the one or the other; and that in all such grants the names of the said adventurers and the several number of each of their shares be expressed; provided alwaies, and it is ordained, that if the said adventurers or any of them do not truly and effectually, with one year next after the sealing of the said grant, pay and discharge all such sums of money wherein by subscription (or otherwise upon notice thereof given from the auditors) they stand indebted to the Company, or if the said adventurers, or any of them having not lawful right, either by purchase from the Company or by assignment from some other former adventurers, within one year after the said grant or by special gift of the Company upon merit preceding in a full quarter court, to so many shares as he or they pretend, do not within one year after the said grant, satisfie and pay to the said Treasurer and Company for every

[25]Blank space.

share so wanting after the rate of twelve pounds ten shillings the share, that then the said grant for so much as concerneth the [26] part and all the shares of the said person so behind and not satisfying as aforesaid shall be utterly void; provided also, and it is ordained, that the grantees shall from time to time during the said seven years make a true certificate to the said Treasurer, Councel and Company from the chief officer or officers of the places respectively, of the number, names, ages, sex, trades and conditions of every such person so transported or shiped, to be entered by the Secretary into a register book for that purpose to be made; that for all persons not comprised in the order next before which during the next seven years after Midsummer day, 1618, shall go into Virginia with intent there to inhabite, if they continue there three years or dye after they are shiped there shall be a grant made of fifty acres for every person upon a first division and as many more upon a second division (the first being peopled), which grants to be made respectively to such persons and their heirs at whose charges the said persons going to inhabite in Virginia shall be transported with reservation of twelve pence yearly rent for every fifty acres to be answered to the said Treasurer and Company and their successors for ever, after the first seven years of every such grant; in which grants a provisoe to be inserted that the grantees shall from time to time during the said seven years make a true certificate to the said Treasurer, Councel and Company, from the chief officer or officers of places respectively, of the number, names, ages, sex, trades and conditions of every such person so transported or shiped, to be entred by the Secretary into a register book for that purpose to be made; that all grants as well of one sort as the other respectively be made with equal favours, and grants of like liberties and immunities as near as may be to the end that all complaint of partiality [or] differencie may be prevented. All which said orders we hereby will and ordain to be

[26]Blank space.

firmly and unvoilably kept and observed and that the inhabitants of Virginia have notice of them for their use and benefit. Lastly, we do hereby require and authorize you, the said Captain George Yeardley and the said Council of Etats, associating with you such other as you shall there find meet, to survey or cause to be survey'd all the lands and territories in Virginia above mentioned and the same to set out by bounds and metes, especially so as that the territories of the said several cities and buroughs and other particular plantations may be conveniently divided and known the one from the other; each survey to be set down distinctly in writing and returned to us under your hands and seals. In witness whereof we have hereunto set our common seal, given in a great and general court of the Council and Company of Adventurers of Virginia held the eighteenth day of November, 1618; and in the years of the reign of our soverain Lord James, by the grace of God, King of England, Scotland, France and Ireland, Defender of the Faith, &c., Vizt. of England, France and Ireland the sixteenth and of Scotland the two and fiftieth. Novr. 18, 1618.

Kingsbury, Vol. III, pp. 98-109.

VIRGINIA COMPANY. INSTRUCTIONS TO THE GOVERNOR AND COUNCIL OF STATE IN VIRGINIA

July 24, 1621

Instructions to the Governor for the time being and Counsell of State in Virginia:

1. First wee requier you in gennerall take into spetiall regard and estimation the service of Almightie God and observance of his divine lawes and that the people in Virginia bee trained up in true religion, god lives and vertue, that ther example may be a meanes to winn the infidells to God: wherin wee pray you especiallie to have in daly rememberance that the patterne which you shall give in your owne persons & in your families wilbee of singular and chief moment whatt may soever itt shall propend. And since our gennerall endeavours and designes have nott yett effected a due establishment of the honor and rights belonginge to the Church and ministerie, wee must requier your most earnest care to advance all things appertayninge thereunto, seriously endeavoring the establishment of due order in administringe of all services according to the usuall forme and discipline of the Church of England and carefullie avoidinge all factious and needlesse novelties tending onlie to the disturbance of peace and unitie; and that such ministers as have been or shalbe sent from time to time may bee respected and mainteined according to the orders made in that behalfe, also for accomodatinge the churches or places for divine service.

2. Wee praie you likewise take care, that the people now ther or hereafter inhabitinge bee kept in due obedience to His Majestie and that they all take the oaths of supremacie and allegiance; and that you provide that justice bee equallie administered to

all His Majesties subjects ther resideing, and as neare as may be after the forme of this realme of England, wherin you are to have a vigilant care to prevent corruption amongst your inferior officers tending to the perverting or delaying of justice; wee praie you also to have espetiall care that no injurie or oppresion bee wrought by the English against any of the natives of that countrie wherby the present peace may be disturbed and ancient quarrells (now buried) might be revived; provided, nevertheles, that the honor of our nation and safety of our people bee still preserved and all maner of insolence committed by the natives be severely and sharpelie punished.

3. Item: that you cause our people to applie themselves to an industrious course of life in followeinge ther buissinesies, each in the several degre and proffession, and that no man bee suffered to live idly, the example wherof might prove pernicious to the rest; in perticular that you bee carefull now in the begining to suppresse too much gaming and above all things that odious vice of drunkenes; and that all kinde of riott both in apparrell & otherwise bee eschewed; and that an edict bee speedily published that no person residing in Virginia (excepting those of the Counsill and heads of hundreds and plantations, ther wives & chilldren) shall weare any gold in ther clothes or any apparrell of silke, untill such time they have itt of the silke ther made by silkewormes & raised by ther owne industry.

4. Item: that you use good prudence that no just cause of offence bee given to any other prince, state or people which are in league or amitie with His Majestie; and that no captaine or other of our Colonie under pretence of trade to the coast of the West Indies bee suffred to saile out with anie vessell ther to robb & spoile wherby to provoke any other nation against us; and that no piratts have cause by . . . accesse to retier with ther purchasses to the coast of Virginia, but that they be severlie punished & ther goods confiscated: for the preventing of which, as

alsoe for securing your selves against all forraigne ennimies, wee require your serious considerations for the speedie errecting of fortresses or blockhouses at the mouth of the river as also for all other manner of needfull fortifications in all places, and to the effecting hereof wee requirer you, as well private persons as hundreds and corporations, bee ratablie proportioned to the performance of certaine dayes worke by the yeare.

5. Item: that the best meanes bee used to draw the better disposed of the natives to converse with our people and labor amongst them with convenient reward that therby they may growe to a likeing and love of civillty and finallie bee brought to the knowledge and love of God and true religion, which may prove also of great strength to our people against the savages or other invadors, whatsoever; and they may bee fitt instruments to assist afterwards in the more gennerall conversion of the heathen people which wee somuch desier.

6. Item: that for the laying of the surer foundation for the said conversion, that each towne, cittie, burrough and other particular plantation bee procured to obtaine to themselves by just meanes a certaine number of the chilldren of the natives to be educated by them in true religion and a civill course of life; of which chilldren the most towardlie boyes in will and graces of nature to bee brought up by them in the first elements of literature so to bee fitted for the colledge, in the fabricke whereof we purpose to proceed assoone as any proffit returned from the tenantes shall enhable us; and doe therfore verie ernestlie requier your uttermost helps aswell for the improveinge of ther labors, as for the true account and returne of the proffitts already due, that so that busines of the colledge may goe forward with which wee doubt not a particular blessing of God will goe a long uppon the Collony ther as wee are assured the love of all good men here to the plantation will therby be encreased.

7. Item: that imediatlie after the gatheringe in of the present yeares cropp by Sir George Yeardlie, wee requier that the land belonging to the place of Governor bee resigned to Sir Francis Wyate and that ther bee delivered to him by Sir George Yeardly the hundred tenants well furnished which wee sent him for the place; and if ther bee any of them wanting, Sir George Yeardly is out of his private to make good the full nomber of a hundred, which wee hope hee will gladlie doe, remembringe our courtesie in the addition of thirtie able persons sent him the former springe to supplie those that wee understood through mortallitie had failed; as also our refusing to accept of his offer to depart [part?] with all the proffitt by the Governors land or tenants, onlie ex-specting his care to cultivate well that land and to uphold that nomber of a hundred tenants for the place.

8. Item: imediatelie upon the expiracion of Sir George Yeardlys goverment on the eighteenth of November next, you shall admitt Sir Francis Wiats commission to bee read, whom accordinglie you shall receave and publish Governor and Captaine Generall, yealding unto his person and place all our respect, honor and observance.

9. Item: the comission for establishing of the Counsell you shall publish uppon the deliverie therof and as speedylie as convenientlie you may to administer the oath of Counsellors unto the severall persons therin named.

10. And forasmuch as ther hath ben in theise late yeares great fault or defect in nott putting in execucion our orders of court and Counsell for the setting upp & upholdinge those staple comodities which are necessarie for the subsisting and encrease of the plantation, which hath happned in part by the our chargeing the Governor with toe much buissnes, wee have uppon espetiall approvement of the industry and sufficiency of George Sandis, Esqr., as also for his faithfulnes and plenarie intelligence

of our intendments and counsells here (wherunto hee hath from time to time bein privie, not only elected and athorised him to bee Treasurer in Virginia, butt also committed to his spetiall and extreordinarie care the execution of all our orders, charters and instructions tending to the setting upp, encrease and maintaininge of the said staple comodities); wee, therefore, requier you that upon all such occationes wherin the said master . . . shall have occation to bee employed, you give him all such countenance, help and power in the execution therof as you would doe to the Governor himselfe if hee were personallie present; and that provition bee made for convenient transporting him from place upon all those occations; we have by order of our quarter court bearing date the second day of May last, allotted unto the place of Treasuror fifteen hundred acres of land and fifty tenants wherof twenty five are now sent and twenty five more are to bee sent the next Spring; to the place of Marshall (wherunto wee have chosen Sir William Neuce) wee have likewise allotted fifteene hundred acres of land and fifty tenantes now provided and furnished and deliverid to the said Sir William Newce to bee transported this present somer; to the place of the Companies Deputie (wherunto wee have formerlie allotted twelve hundred acres and forty men) wee have added three hundred acres of land and tenn tenants more to bee sent the next springe; to the phisitions place wee have allotted twenty tenantes sent last spring and five hundred acres of land; to the Secretarie, five hundred acres of land and twenty tenantes sent out the last springe; for the accomateinge of which severall persons in ther places & offices in the best manner according to our promises, furtherance that in you lieth.

11. Item: wee pray you likewise with convenient speed to reveive the commissiones formerlie directed to Sir George Yeardly, then Governor, and to the Counsell of State ther beareinge date the 18 of November, 1618, conteining the lawes & orders for dividing

the citties and burroughs with ther land and people, and sondrie other particularities for the well settling of that State. And haveing sent you coppies of all such instructions, letters, charters & directions as have here before been sent from time to time, wee pray you to peruse them all and what soever you shall find not contrarie to any of theise instructions and requisite for the behouf of Collonie ther or of the Companie here, wee wish you to observe itt as though the same were here particularly inserted. Also all orders of courtes that shall bee certified uppon peticions or otherwise, under the attest of our Secretaries hand referred unto the Governor or Counsell ther, wee pray you see that a due course bee taken accordinglie to doe the partie whome it shall concerne right and justice, no lesse then if they had been particularly here by name commended unto you.

12. Item: that the captaines and heades of everie particular plantation or hundreds, as likewise everie cheif officer that hath people under his charge, deliver severall catalogues at one of the fower quarter sessions of the Counsell yearly as well of the severall names, conditions and qualities of those that bee liveing, as also of those that bee dead, and likewise of the mariages and christnings hapninge with that place; and that the personall goods and estate of the partie deceased bee carefullie keptt & reserved to the rightt owners therof; and lastlie that a list bee kept of the nomber of all sorts of cattell in each particular burrough or plantation; and that you cause the Secretarie once everie yeare to returne us hether a perfect coppie of all the premisses.

13. Item: that whereas the principall hope of the plantacion dependes much on the prosperity of particular Colonies or hundreds, itt wilbe verie necessarie that in case of the death or other misaccidents of the chief heads of those Colonies, you take into your carefull regaurd the conservation of the bodie and sinews

of that plantation united, preserving the remaines by the best meanes that either industry or charity can effect.

14. Item: that according to His Majesties gratious advise and the desire & expectacion of the whole state here, you draw the people from the excessive planting of tobacco and that, according to a late order of court in that behalfe made the thirteenth of June last, you suffer them not to plaint in one yeare alone one hundred waight tobacco the head, that is the person; and that you do provide by some generall course to bee held amongst them that they apply themselves to the soweing and planting of corne in good plentie that ther may bee alwaies a large proportion not onlie for their owne use, but store also for such as in great multitudes wee hope yearly to send; likewise by the same generall course to cause the generall inhabitants and households to enclose by pale & strong fences some fitting portion of our land for the keping of cowes, tame swine and poultrie; and for the making all due provitiones for the encrease & preservation of the bread of all sorts of cattle, and in particular kine, wherof wee thinke itt most unfitt that any should bee as yett killed and requier your vigilent care for the inhibiting thereof.

15. Item: after corne, wee comend unto your care the matter of silke which his Majesty heretofore espetially to commended unto us and out of his owne store hath moste gratiouslie been pleased often to furnish our Company with seed: in supply of which more hath bin since sent and a greater quantitie shall likewise followe hereafter as soone as itt shall come to our hands. Wee requier therfore that you cause in everie particular plantation great nomber of mulbery trees to bee plainted neare ther dwellings, and such as are already groweing to bee preserved for planting, of which many excellent bookes have binn already sent in December last, unto which wee referr you for your better direction therin, as also to divers French and other experienced

men, late sent & procured at extraordinarie charge, of whose generall subsistence wee expect your assidious care.

16. Item: silke grasse, being a comoditie of spetiall hope and much use, not with standing through negligence and want of experience, it hath lately been declared to bee full of difficullty and hazard both in growcing and curing, yett we doe especially recomend unto your care and that you direct some good way to bring it to perfection by experimenting the soiles, the seasons and true maner of cultivating of itt, being confident that that which growes so naturally in those parts will much more by art and industry bee at lenght brought to perfection, and being many wayes so usefull will bring great honor an [and?] proffitt unto the action.

17. Item: wee doe also especially recommend unto you the planting of vines in aboundance and that the vignerons sent with so great charge to the Company bee fairely & carefullie provided for.

18. Item: wee requier also that all sorts of artsmen be employed in ther severall trades and that store of aprentizes bee placed & held to learne ther occupations, especially those that are most usefull or most comodious; and that you duely consider the quallities and trades of all those people sent over for the Companies or any of the Collonies servis & that you cause them to bee held to ther trades and occupations wherin ther are like to deserve & win most bennifitt; and not to suffer them to forsake ther former occupacions for planting tobacco or such uselesse comodities. And here wee earnestly commend unto your care the Dutchemen sent for the erecting of sawing mills, a worke most necessarie since the materialls for howsing and shipping can not otherwise without much more troble, paines and charge bee provided;& although wee have received some notice that fitting places for ther works and not ther easilie found out, yett wee hope that dillegence fitting to bee used in a case of so gen-

erall benifitt hath discoverid how to make use of ther skills by this time. Nor doe wee here apprehend any difficullty of finding accomodation for that purpose about the falls or towards the heads of some river or brookes by the station, wherof timber may be brought unto them verie easili and by the current of the river the plankes or boords sawen may bee transported for the generall use of all or the greatest part of our people.

19. Item: that your corne mills bee presentlie erected and pupliqe bakehowses in everie burrough bee built with all speed and dilligence.

20. Item: that all apparent or proved contracts made in England or in Virginia betweene the owners of land in Virginia and ther tenants or servants be truly performed and the breach of them reformed by due punishment as justice shall requier.

21. Item: that you suffer no crafty or advantageous meanes to bee used to entice a way the tenants or servants of any particular plantacion from the place they are . . . ceited and that all offenders herein bee severlie punished and the partie drawne away bee returned to ther former place.

[22]. Wee commend unto your especiall regard the providing for such persons as have already bin sent or are now or shall be hereafter entertained for the erecting of iron works; that all possible meanes bee used for ther encouradgment & for the performing of generall contracts here made with the Company wherby justice unto them and profitt to the plantation may arise. And whereas Mr. John Berkly hath bin approved unto us here by extreordinary recommendations to bee industrious and intelligent gentleman many ways, butt espetially for iron works, wee decier hee & his company may bee cherished by you and supported by the helpe of the whole Colonie if need shall requier, therby to enhable him to perfect that worke wherupon the Company have already expended great somes of money & itt is a com[modity]

so necessarie as few other are to bee valewed in comparrison therof. Upon the successe therof also, mèns eyes are generally fixed & therfore if itt should now (as by former misaccident or negligence) fall to the ground, ther were little hope that ever they would bee revived againe; and whereas wee have bin so circomspect as to contraict with many masters severally for the erecting of the said works, wherby wee hoped though some miscarried or failled others should have proceeded; if by want of workes or necessarie materialls the said masters cannot for present bee seatted or enjoy the conditions of ther contraicts, wee thinke fitt you should accomodate them according to ther several habillities in some secondarie or subordinarie places of assistance to Mr. Berkly, or when another worke may be advanced to worke them over that, according (as neere as may bee) to ther contraictes made here with the Company, wherby this worke of so great consequence & generall expectacion, infinitt com[modity] & unspeakeable benifitt to the plantacion may bee dilligentlie prosecuted & upheld.

23. Item: salt, pich and tarr, soape ashes, &c., often recommended and sett up, and for which fittinge men & matterialles have been sent to the great charge of the Company and yett daylie complaints come to us of the want of them, wee desier you will now prosecute and further with all dilligence & care.

24. Item: your makeing of oile of wallnuts, your employing your apothecaries in distilling of hott waters out of your lees of beere and searching after minierall dyes, gummes, druggs, and the like things, wee desier you not to forgett and good quanteties of all sorts to send us by all shipps.

25. Item: since wee have conceaved itt most fitting to ordaine that a small quantety of tobacco shall bee plainted or cherished in Virginia, wee hold itt verie necessarie to use all possible care that the proporcion limmitted may bee improved in goodnes as

much as may bee; and therefore that some good order bee taken to see itt well cured and duely ordred that bringing itt into request may cause any certaine benifitt to the planters.

26. Item: that due proceeding bee used in the erection of those howses appointed for lodgeing of new men upon ther landing, according to former directions; and that from time to time a course bee taken for ther repaire, cleane & neat; keeping likewise, for comon store, howses in convenient places as well for other needs necessary provitions, as upper roomes for conservation of a proportion of gounpouder ready for use.

27. Item: whereas wee have many times found losse & interuption in our buissines through want of frequent relacion from Virginia, wee therefore requier you att least to make a quarterly dispatch unto us, the duplicate wherof to bee duely sentt by the next oppertunitie of shipping after.

28. Item: whereas Capt. William Norton and certaine Itallians, now by the general Company and other worthy minded adventures att a verie great charge, sent for the erecting of a glasse furnace in Virginia, wee hartilie desire you to afford them all favor possible. And in particular that the guesthowses built by Leftenant Whitakers bee allowed them for ther habitacion till they may convenientlie provide themselves of ther owne; and that all orders given them from hence bee exactlie putt in execucion.

29. Item: a gentleman's great dilligence in our affaires, accompaned with extreordinarie capacity and judgement, haveing proceeded the treatise of the buissnes belonging to the plantacion, approved by us to bee full of excllent observances for those that are emmenly employd in Virginia, as well for us here, wee sent a coppy to ly amongst the records of your Counsell from whence, from the often veiw of former passadgs, wee wish every Counsellor may make permanent instructions, and no doubt

much helps and furtherance may bee produced in most occasiones for the advancement of the plantacion.

30. Item: that ther be espetiall care taken both of generall and particular survaies wherby not onlie a true mapp and face of the whole country, costs, creeks, rivers, highe ground & lowe ground, &c., may bee exactlie discoverid, but also the boundaries of the severall hundreds and plantacions, with the perticuler directions in them bee perfectlie sett forth from time to time, mainetained to prevent therby future differences that arise upon questions of possestion, wherin also itt may be fitting and moste usefull to posteritie to cast an imaginarie eye and view, wher and which way the grand highewayes may bee like to strike and passe through the dominions; in which course the hard mountaines, the fords, the places for bridges, &c., may nott unfittlie bee considered; for performance of all which the premises (and for the better sattisfaction) of the planters, whoe have so often required ther lands may bee devided and bounded, wee have now sent and furnished out Mr. William Cleyburne, gentleman, recomended unto us as very [fitt] in the art of surveying.

31. Item: the oppressing and imoderate fees heretofore exacted in Virginia by divers officers in valuacion of ther paines & travell for the Colonies service have partlie occationed the settling a competent revenue to arrise therby tenants to everie cheif officer; wee now forbidd that officer so provided for, or otherwise by allotted parts out of the common profitt recompenced, doe take any other fees for execution of ther severall places either directly or indirectly; neverthelesse, that clarks & such like may have a reward for ther dilligence, wee require you by order to sett downe some small proportion for passes, warrants, copies of orders, seales, &c., or proportionably to the merits of servants paines and attendance.

32. Item: the Governor & Counsell assembled within a short

time after the arivall of this shipp are to sett downe the fittest months after ther quarterlie meeting of the Counsell of State according to the seasons and to fitting meanes for ther entertayment, together with regaurd of the best ease and benifitt of the people, that shall have occasion to addresse themselves unto the Counsell, either for justice or direction; considering also the times of making ther dispathes to England, according to the oppertunities of shiping ther comeing or goeing.

33. That the Governor for the time being in or about the foresaid time doe summon by an officer appointed for that purpose the Counsell of State to appeare at a day and to bee together for the space of one whole month or more if need shall requier to advise & consult upon matter of Counsell of State and of the generall affaires of the Colonie, and as ther shalbee cause to order and determine the greater causes of consequence or such matter as shall growe or arise within the Colonie, either by reference or judgment; and that free accesse bee permitted to all suiters to make knowne ther perticuler grevances, bee itt against what person soever. And if the plaint appeare to bee important, to record the same ther & to returne a coppy ther of together with the report of your proceeding therin.

34. As also to keepe a perfect register of all the acts of each quarter sessions duely and orderlie and therof to returne a perfect transcript unto us by the first oppertunitie of shipping from time to time. And that at everie sessions you cause all instructions and charters that are already or shall hereafter bee sent from hence to bee read and so from sessions to sessions untill our directory shall bee fullie executed.

35. Item. in case of the Governor death or removall or suspen cion by order from hence untill other direction from us can come, wee requier that the Counsell or major part of them then residing in Virginia doe imedialie assemble themselves and within fourteene dayes or sooner from out of ther body to elect one

to supplie the place for the time; and to preserve the state of bussinesse still in the same current that it was.

36. The relation of which act of Counsell wee will you send us with as much speede as may bee, and if ther should bee an unexpected division in the voices of the counsell that a just halfe should bee willing to elect one and the other halfe desirous of another, then wee will that election bee made of the Leftennant Governor; and in his absence or necessarie cause of declining the Marshall, and in case of his default or such refusall then the Treasurer, then one of the two deputies or the other till the place of Governor be settled in on [one] of our said cheif officers.

37. Item: whereas ther hath bin severall directions given to the former Governor for fixing the tenants uppon the lands as well belonging to the Governor place as other the officers seated by the Governor, which uppon pretences hath bin allowed and neglected and the men lett out to the heir; wee requier you that hereafter no officer bee permitted to lett out his tenants, butt settle them uppon the lands sett out for his place, enjoining them to enclose gardens, build howses, deviding them into families or societies, to place them upon the land appropriated to his office, excepting onlie the Counsell shall have power to make a convenient order at one of the quarter sessions to dispence with this article for the space of six months & that in case onlie of extreeme necessitie.

38. Item: the Governor, onlie for the time being, shall summon Counsells and sine warrants & execute or give athoritie for execution of the Counsells orders, except in cases which seeme to appertaine to the imediate execucions of Liftenant Generall, Marshall, Tresuror, or deputies, wherin according to ther severall comissions or by a conceaved order from a quarter counsell the officers are severallie directed and authorised.

39. The Governor for the time being shall have absolute power

and authoritie according to the implicacion of his perticular commission to direct, determine and punish at his good discretion any emergent buissnes, neglect or contempt of authority in any kind or what soever negligence or contempt may bee found in any person ther residing or being, except only those of the Counsell for ther on persons whoe are in such cases to bee summoned to appeare at the next quarter session of the Counsell holdne ther abide ther censure; in the meane time if the Governor shall thinke itt may concerne either the quiett of that state to proceed more speedily with such an offendor, itt shall bee lawful to summon a Counsell extreordinarie, wherat six of the Counsell at lest are to bee present with the said Governor and by the main parte of ther voices committ any Counsellor to saife custody or upon baile to appere and abide the order of the nextt quarter counsell.

40. Everie order and decree of the Counsell of State shalbe concluded by the major parte of voices at that Assembly, wherin the Governor for the time being is to have a casting voice if the nomber of Counsellors should bee even or should bee equally devided in oppinnion; neverthelesse reserving to the said Governor a negative voice att any Generall Assembly according to a former comission granted.[26]

41. Item: wee pray you likewise to take into your care the protexcion of the people, that they suffer no wrong by the engrossing commodity & forestalling the marketts, butt preserve them open for all men freely or indifferently to buy or sell.

42. Item: wee requier you expecially to see the publicke labors to bee from time to time equally charged & burdned for the people that one mans tenants bee nott favored above others or officers tenants favored more then those of the puplique; and to the end those services may fall as easy to all ports as may bee, wee thinke in the punishment of all enormus misdemeanors,

[26]One of the few references to the *Commission,* not the "Instructions", to Yeardley, authorizing a General Assembly.

&c., ill deservers bee condemned to a nomber of days works for puplique use & building, or to finnishing of a fence or dike, or to cariage or roweing according to the meritt of the offence.

43. Item: where as the Right Honourable the Earle of Pembroke with divers his associates have undertaken to plaint thirty thousand acres of land in Virginia, we therfore intreat you to make choice of the best seate on that river that is not yett inhabited; and herin to take the advise of Mr. Leech, whoe now goes over to veiw the cuntrie and to bee enployd in that plantacion which being sett out wee desier to be informed therof.

44. Item: as wee hold itt most necessarie that you provide for the generall safety and securing of your selves and estats together, so doe wee conceave it a matter of exceeding great advantage & incouragment to discover everie day farther by the sea coast and within land about which wee requier you to conceave a fitting course from time espetiallie to find good fishing betweene James river and Cape Cod or any wher within our limmittes wherin wee suppose the new trade of commodities found wilbe like to recompence the troble and charge bestowed therin, for wee are certainely informed that the Dutchmen within 20 or 30 leagues of your plantacion steile a trade for furrs, &c., to ther verie great gaine & content.

45. Item: for as much as planting of staple commodities is useuallie much advanced by example taken one from another, wee expect that the cheif officers by ther owne particular employment of ther people & land, & setting forth the benifitts & hopes of such endeavors, shall exceedinglie advance the state of commodity and trade.

46. Item: wee doe moreover requier that according to your oaths and severall charges your thoughts & endeavors be unanimouslie employed for performance of our instructions in generall, & particuler that chieflie aiminge at the establishment of the Colonie

your selves & all of us that have endeavorid therein may bee comforted in a happie apparence of prosperity of the plantacion which wilbe glorious before God and infinitt honor, strenght & profitt to our King & Cuntry.

47. Lastly wee pray you that no shipp that now or at any time wee shall send at the companies charge to Virginia bee suffered to stay ther above thirty dayes for avoiding of charge which hath heretofore grown uppon long voydges in freight & wages & that you suffer not in the said shipps any goods provicions sent thither to bee brought from thence againe by any marriners, passengers or others uppon paine of some punishment to be inflicted upon them; and although the infancy of the plantacion may nott some time afford the more valuable comodities to freight the shipps home uppon so short a stay, yett wee suppose that a prudent course & preperacion may at last afford them choice timber as clear walnutt or some other such lesse valueable commodity to add to ther lading which will yeild more profitt to the Companie with the shipps quicke returne then is useually raised by ther best comodities when longer accompt for freightt hath drawne on a further charge. Given under the Counsell seale the fower and twentith day of Julie, 1621; and in the yeare of the raign of our soveraigne Lord James, by the grace of God of England, Scotland, France and Ireland, Defender of the faith, &c., that is to say of England, France and Ireland the nineteenth and Scottland the fower and fiftith.

Signed by the Earl of Southampton

Sir Edwin Sandis	Mr. Nicholas Ferrar
Mr. John Davers	Doctor Anthony
Mr. John Ferrar, deputy	Doctor Willliamson
Mr. Thomas Gibbs	Doctor Galston
Mr. Sam Wrote	Mr. George Sandys

Kingsbury, Vol. III, pp. 468-482.

TREASURER AND COMPANY. AN ORDINANCE AND CONSTITUTION FOR COUNCIL AND ASSEMBLY IN VIRGINIA

July 24, 1621

To all people to whom these presents shall come, bee seen or heard, the Treasuror, Council and Company of Adventurers and Planters of the Citty of London for the First Collony in Virginia send greeting: knowe yee that wee, the said Treasuror, Counsell and Company, takeing into our carefull consideracion the present state of the said Colony in Virginia, and intending by the Devine assistance to settle such a forme of government ther as may bee to the greatest benifitt and comfort of the people and wherby all injustice, grevance and oppression may bee prevented and kept of as much as is possible from the said Colony, have thought fitt to make our entrance by ordaining & establishing such supreame Counsells as may not only bee assisting to the Governor for the time being in administracion of justice and the executing of other duties to his office belonging, but also by ther vigilent care & prudence may provide as well for remedy of all inconveniencies groweing from time to time as also for the advancing of encrease, strength, stabillitie and prosperitie of the said Colony:

Wee therefore, the said Treasuror, Counsell and Company, by authoritie directed to us from His Majestie under his Great Seale, upon mature deliberacion doe hereby order & declare that from hence forward ther bee towe supreame Counsells in Virginia for the better government of the said Colony as aforesaid: the one of which Counsells to bee called the Counsell of State and whose office shall cheiflie bee assisting, wth ther care, advise & circumspection, to the said Governor; shall be chosen, nominated, placed and displaced from time to time by us, the said Treasurer, Counsell & Company and our successors; which Counsell of State shall consiste for the present onlie of those persons whose names are here inserted, vizt.: Sir Francis Wyatt, Gov ernor of Virginia; Captaine Francis West; Sir George Yeardley, Knight; Sir William Newce, Knight, Marshall of Virginia; Mr. George Sandys, Tresuror; Mr. George Thorpe, Deputy of the Colledge; Captaine Thomas Newce, Deputy for the Company; Mr. Christopher Davison, Secretarie; Doctor Potts, Phesition to the Company; Mr. Paulet; Mr. Leech; Captaine Nathaniell Powell; Mr. Roger Smith; Mr. John Berkley; Mr. John Rolfe; Mr. Ralfe Hamer; Mr. John Pountus; Mr. Michael Lapworth; Mr. Harwood; [and] Mr. Samuel Macocke. Which said Counsellors and Counsell wee earnestlie pray & desier, and in His Majesties name strictlie charge and command, that all factious parcialties and sinister respects laid aside, they bend ther care and endeavors to assist the said Governor first and principallie in advancement of the honor and service of Almightie God and the enlargement of His kingdome amongste those heathen people; and next in the erecting of the said Colonie in one obedience to His Majestie and all lawful authoritie from His Majestis dirived; and lastlie in maitaining the said people in justice and Christian conversation among themselves and in strength and habillitie to wth stand ther ennimies. And this Counsell is to bee alwaies, or for the most part, residing about or neere the said Governor. The other Counsell, more generall, to bee called by the Governor, and yeerly, of course, & no oftner but for very extreordinarie & important occasions, shall consist for present of the said Counsell of State and of tow burgesses out of every towne, hunder [hundred] and other particuler plantacion to bee respetially chosen by the inhabitants. Which Counsell shalbee called the Generall Assemblie, wherein as also in the said Counsell of State, all matters shall be decided, determined & ordered by the greater part of the voices then present, reserveing alwaies to the Governor a negative voice. And this Generall Assembly shall have free power to treat, consult & conclude as well of all emergent occasions concerning the puplique weale of the said Colony and evrie parte therof as also to make, ordeine

& enact such generall lawes & orders for the behoof of the said Colony and the good govermt therof as shall time to time appeare necessarie or requisite. Wherin as in all other things wee requier the said Gennerall Assembly, as also the said Counsell of State, to imitate and followe the policy of the forme of goverment, lawes, custome, manners of loyall and other administracion of justice used in the realme of England, as neere as may bee even as ourselves by His Majesties lettres patents are required; provided that noe lawes or ordinance made in the said Generall Assembly shalbe and continew in force and validitie, unlese the same shalbe sollemlie ratified and confirmed in a generall greater court of the said court here in England and so ratified and returned to them under our seale. It being our intent to affoord the like measure also unto the said Colony that after the goverment of the [said Colony, shall once have been well framed & settled accordingly, which is to be done by us as by authoritie derived from] his Majestie and the sa[me shall] have bene soe by us declared, no orders of our court afterwarde shall binde [the said] Colony unles they bee ratified in like manner in ther Generall Assembly.

In wittnes wherof wee have hereunto sett our common seale the 24th day of [July] 1621, and in the yeare of the raigne of our governoure, Lord James by the . . . of God of England, Scotland, France & Ireland, King, Defendor of the . . . vizt., of England, France and Scotland the nineteenth and of Scotland the fower and fiftieth.

Kingsbury, Vol. III, pp. 482-484. Stith, Appendix, pp. 32-34.

www.ingramcontent.com/pod-product-compliance
Ingram Content Group UK Ltd.
Pitfield, Milton Keynes, MK11 3LW, UK
UKHW021053270726
13967UKWH00012B/643